Of Reason and Love:

The Life and Works of Marie von Ebner-Eschenbach

Studies in Austrian Literature, Culture, and Thought

Carl Steiner

Of Reason and Love:

The Life and Works of

Marie von Ebner-Eschenbach

(1830-1916)

Ariadne Press

PT
1853
.Z5
S74
1994

Ariadne Press would like to express its appreciation to the Austrian Cultural Institute, New York for assistance in publishing this book.

Library of Congress Cataloging-in-Publication Data

Steiner, Carl, 1927-
    Of reason and love : the life and works of Marie von
Ebner-Eschenbach (1830-1916) / Carl Steiner.
        p.   cm. -- (Studies in Austrian literature,
culture, and thought)
    Includes bibliographical references and index.
    ISBN 0-929497-77-5
    1. Ebner-Eschenbach, Marie von, 1830-1916.
2. Authors, Austrian--19th century--Biography.
I. Title. II. Series
PT1853.Z5S74   1994
833'.8--dc20
[B]   93-26091
                                              CIP

Cover design:
Art Director and Designer: George McGinnis

28505065

In Memory of My Mother

Anna Amalia Steiner,

Née Scholz-Maxera,

Born in Vienna, Austria,

On March 12, 1902,

of German and Moravian

Forebears

CONTENTS

INTRODUCTION

Marie von Ebner-Eschenbach was the foremost woman writer of the Realist period in German letters in the second half of the nineteenth century and one of the period's most widely respected and honored literary figures. She can still be considered the *grande dame* of Austrian literature today. It is an uncanny historical coincidence that her life span, extending from 1830 to 1916, equalled that of Franz Joseph I, the last prominent Austrian emperor. However, Marie von Ebner-Eschenbach did not reflect the attitudes and sentiments of the moribund Austrian aristocracy, of which she was a leading member. On the contrary, she was a strong and outspoken critic of its excesses and weaknesses. Although she considered the labor-intensive machines, the dismal factories, the growing cities, the suffering proletariat, and the social miseries associated with these new developments inappropriate topics and themes for poetry and imaginative literature and disagreed with many aims and tenets of literary Naturalism, she opened her heart and mind to the world and the people around her and dealt with the underlying social and political currents of the era. Most significantly, perhaps, she approached and presented the multifaceted cultural and political difficulties confronting her age from the woman's point of view.

It is the intention of this study to present in the initial chapter a comprehensive picture of her life and to utilize the next three chapters for a critical presentation and analysis of her writings. The concluding chapter will deal with her timeless and lasting contributions to literature, thought, and social criticism. She has left us a rich legacy and a broad spectrum of literary works, consisting of aphorisms, parables, poems, and plays as well as fairy tales, shorter narratives, novellas, and novels. My approach to her oeuvre will be basically chronological and biographical. Since she did not write her works in a self-imposed sociopolitical vacuum, the social and historical backgrounds of the age will consistently be involved. Inasmuch as she honed her writing skills in all major literary genres, an attempt will have to be made to group her work as much as is possible along generic lines as well. In this endeavor some philological underpinning is necessary for clarification and to spare the reader the chore of referring to reference works for necessary background information. This study is primarily intended for the English-speaking world, where her writings are practically unknown. I will therefore also include plot summaries whenever and wherever they are considered necessary as a prerequisite to the analytical and critical discussions. Key extracts from the works of Marie von Ebner-Eschenbach will be given to allow the reader to form his or her independent judgment of the power, persuasiveness, and beauty of her style. Since it must be assumed that many readers of this monograph will not be conversant with German, these as well as all other quotations from German texts will be translated into English.

I am indebted to Mrs. Margrit B. Krewson, the German and Dutch specialist of the Library of Congress, for her invaluable help in establishing a basic Ebner-Eschenbach bibliography. My considerable appreciation also extends to the dedicated staff of the Gelman Library of the George Washington University and especially to Dr. Quadir Amiryar, whose department of interlibrary loans was most helpful in making many of the needed texts available to me. Special gratitude is owed to Mrs. Carol Chamberlain, who undertook the considerable task of proofreading my manuscript. To my wife, Ruth M. Steiner, I am deeply beholden for her patient and understanding support of this undertaking during the many months of its writing. I have dedicated the monograph to my dear mother in everlasting devotion, whose lifelong love of late nineteenth-century *Frauenliteratur* (women's literature) was my primary source of inspiration.

Chapter I

A WOMAN'S VOICE

To call the nineteenth century a stereotypical "man's world" is no overstatement. Three men, in effect—Queen Victoria notwithstanding—dominated its unfolding and direction in Europe, if not in the world, at that time in human history: Napoleon, Metternich, and Bismarck. Although they were cultured and refined men by modern standards, they shared also certain basic characteristics with the dictators and warlords of our own age. They believed in the ruthless application of power and coercion in domestic and international affairs, and they were firmly convinced that their policies could not succeed unless they were in complete control of the events they helped unfold. As a consequence they were strong adherents and firm practitioners of Machiavellian principles. Ultimately, they thought of themselves as sole arbiters of the fate of their people and were supremely confident of their ability as policy and decision makers.

Austria, the heartland of Europe, was strongly affected by all three of these men and their policies. Its own chancellor, although not a native son, Prince Klemens von Metternich— who was to imprint his name on the epoch from 1815 to 1848—tried in vain to restore the country to its earlier political importance and greatness. The Age of Restoration, which he initiated in 1815 in the aftermath of the glittering Congress of Vienna, over which he also presided, was only a limited and, viewed in retrospect, temporary success. It ended abruptly and violently in the revolution of 1848, which failed, however, to reinvigorate the weakened and ever more decrepit Danube monarchy in its endeavor to gain a much-needed long range and durable lease on life.

There were, to be sure, notable beginnings and changes at work, which—at the time—showed promise and gave much hope for new vigor and future stability. A young and handsome emperor, the eighteen-year-old Franz Joseph, ascended to the Habsburg throne to give the anticipated new age in a seemingly renewed empire symbolic freshness. His was to become one of the longest reigns of any monarch in all of recorded history. He was emperor of Austria and king of Hungary for sixty-eight years. Popular and venerated by nearly three generations of his subjects, he was the ruling monarch of the Danube empire from 1848 to 1916.[1] Not that his reign unfolded without difficulties and numerous public and personal defeats. Early in his long rule, in 1868, the single monarchical entity of Austria became the dual monarchy of Austria-Hungary, raising the expectations of other national and ethnic minorities under the Habsburg umbrella— primarily the Czechs and Poles—for equal political recognition, treatment, and eventual independence.

The social compact in nineteenth-century Austria was not exceptionally backward by Central and Western European standards, but then again, neither was it conspicuously forward looking. Yet compared with Eastern Europe, much of which Austria tried to dominate at the time, and to the Russian empire, with which it competed politically and strategically for hegemony in these parts, it was a fountain of progress.[2] Still, a woman's place in all social strata of Austrian society was rather strictly proscribed and limited to family, home, and church activities. This social consensus, if not ingrained mode of behavior or even law, was much more pronounced, visible, and universally observed in Austrian provincial life than it was in the social mores of the capital city of Vienna. There, as in other cultural centers of Central and Western Europe, the condition of women improved in a slow but steady movement toward assimilation. This trend, to be sure, was much more visible and pronounced in the upper strata of society. But in general Austrian society, as elsewhere, this slowly unfolding development did not seriously threaten the long-established tradition of male domination, which was based on the assumption that the male segment of the human species was uniquely endowed by nature with superior reasoning capacity and the wherewithal to engage in the intellectual pursuits of truth and beauty. Most people, including women, believed that the woman was better equipped to inspire her male counterpart to pursue his perennial quest toward attaining these higher goals than making a deliberate effort to accomplish these aims on her own. Even the celebrated German poet Goethe had subscribed to these ideas and had given them their perhaps noblest expression in his *Faust,* which ends with the often cited words: "The eternal feminine / Moves us upward."[3] This poetic statement, universally admired and respected in all German-speaking countries, was a vast improvement over the earlier notions of women's inferiority vis-à-vis their male counterparts which were still upheld in strict Catholic tradition and reinforced by church doctrine throughout the realm.[4]

In Western Europe, especially in France and England, the slowly intensifying movement on the part of women toward the attainment of greater freedom and independence in the economic, political, and juridical spheres had emerged with the advent of the French Revolution—brought about by the writings of French and English writers and philosophers—and began thereafter to spread slowly in the German-speaking lands. There it was at first primarily a question of education.

The schools of higher learning simply did not want to admit women. In this regard the situation of women was similar to that of the Jews in the empire. Since they were denied entry into the schools of higher learning, they had to rely very heavily on the home and on the places of worship for their education. For the vast majority of women the latter meant, of course, the churches. These circumstances favored the privileged classes, that is to say, the aristocracy and the wealthy merchants and artisans. But even the privileged women among them could not gain entry into the professions for lack of a university education. Thus women were caught in a vicious cycle. It was only after the Revolution of 1848 that the bastions of male domination began to be breached. Not until 1865, though, were women able to organize their efforts toward genuine assimilation in Leipzig—Germany's *Klein-Paris* (Small Paris) and one of the country's most liberal cities—by founding the *Allgemeine Deutsche Frauenverein* (Public Society for German Women).[5] Conditions in Austria lagged behind.

Although the women's emancipation movement in Austria can be said to have started only one year later with the establishment of the *Wiener Frauenerwerbsverein* (Organization of Viennese Working Women) in 1866, its expansion was seriously stymied by its lower to middle class origins. Similar clubs followed the early lead of the *Wiener Frauenerwerbsverein* and expanded into such areas as job orientation, female professionalism, consumer affairs, and recognition of home making as a profession. All these efforts, however, lacked a strong, nationally recognized umbrella organization encompassing Austrian women in general. They heavily relied on private initiatives aiming primarily to bring about breakthroughs in the areas of education and professional training. Women of the upper social strata, especially those of noble birth, had different and less pressing agendas. Not being forced into productive labor by virtue of their birth, their primary emancipatory concerns dealt with equality in their respective households and the opportunity to be able to enter the higher professions through the gates of institutions of higher learning, hitherto closed to them.[6]

Marie von Ebner-Eschenbach was born into this slowly evolving social milieu on September 13, 1830, as the second daughter of Baron Franz Dubsky and his wife Marie, née Baroness von Vockel, in Zdislawitz in the Austrian crownland of Moravia. Her full name was Marie Dubsky von Třembomyslic. Her mother died sixteen days after her birth, leaving behind another child as well, Marie's older sister Friederike. This sister was fourteen months of age, Marie barely two weeks old when their mother died of apoplexy. Fortunately, the tragic death of her mother—whose nearly saintly picture was preserved for Marie by old and devoted servants who had known and revered her—did not leave a deep and injurious void in the growing child's psyche. Left motherless almost immediately after birth, Marie was indeed fortunate to be affectionately cared for by two future stepmothers in years to come. In addition, Grandmother Vockel, her mother's stepmother, and Aunt Helene, her father's sister, who were in charge of the Dubsky household at intermittent periods, showed her much love and understanding.

Franz von Dubsky, Marie's father, was the offspring of old Bohemian nobility. The name first appeared in an old chronicle in 1406 in descriptive embellishment as Knight Wilhelm Dubsky von Třembomyslic, Feudal Lord of the Royal Castle Karlstein. Two hundred years later Emperor Rudolf II raised another Wilhelm Dubsky, who had become a wealthy landowner through marriage, to the rank of baron. The latter became involved eleven years later, however, in a rebellion against the emperor and after the Battle of White Mountain was condemned to forfeit his entire fortune. Although Fortuna was to smile on him again, he experienced several ups and downs in his lifetime. Marie's father, the retired major Franz Dubsky, had returned from the War of Liberation against Napoleon with severe injuries that left him partly disabled. He had been gravely wounded in battle in 1814 and taken prisoner by the French. His disabilities forced him to end his military career two years after the war. In 1829 he married the young Baroness Marie Vockel, heiress of Zdislawitz. Her father, the Protestant Baron Vockel, had moved from his native Saxony to Catholic Austria to manage the run-down Zdislawitz estate which he had purchased earlier. When he left it to his daughter Marie through inheritance, it was by all accounts a showplace. The newly married couple took up permanent residence there, after Franz Dubsky had served intermittently as a chamberlain to Emperor Franz I, and assumed the lifestyle of propertied country nobility. Franz Dubsky and Marie Vockel were said to have had two opposite personalities. He was known as a volatile and belligerent person. Politically, he was antiliberal. People described him as a "knight of truth," an overly blunt and outspoken individual. She was a gentle type and was loved and revered by everybody—family, friends, acquaintances, and servants. They all admired her as a calm woman of harmony and congeniality.[7]

Zdislawitz, where Marie was to spend most of her childhood and her subsequent youth, was an imposing Moravian castle and country estate in the vicinity of the small town of Kremsier. Not surprisingly, considering the times and the locale, the relationship between the aristocratic owners and the servants and employees, who were largely of local peasant stock, was much closer to reflecting conditions of this sort in the middle ages than anticipating the coming of a new age of social changes and liberalization. The regimen in the home and on the fields was strict and hierarchical. Occasional beatings of field workers by overseers were not uncommon, as Marie was to discover to her horror while growing up there. She reflected on one such incident years later in her autobiographical essay *Aus meinen Kinder- und Lehrjahren* (From My Childhood and Apprenticeship Years).[8] From this essay, the first of a number in which she practices the skill of bringing back to life the recollections of her childhood, we also learn that she was a bit on the wild side in her formative years for a girl of her social standing, averse to learning, reading, knitting, and other such activities considered to be appropriate. Unable to develop any relationship —other than that of hearsay—with her natural mother, she became attached to her first stepmother Eugénie, née Baroness von Bartenstein, and grew extremely fond of her over the years. But the tragedy of early death repeated itself. "Maman Eugénie," as the children were to call her affectionately, died in 1837 soon after giving birth to a child, which tragically also succumbed to death. Family history was to repeat itself. Marie's father, the baron, was grief-stricken once more but eventually resolved to live on and, several years later, married again. By her own account Marie also developed a good relationship over the years with her second stepmother Xaverine, a born Countess of Kolowrat. Yet Marie's early marriage to a much older cousin casts some doubt on this contention. In any case this highly cultured woman became head of the Dubsky household during the remainder of Marie's girlhood. All the children in the family, including two younger brothers, were looked after by a faithful Czech nanny by the name of Josefa Navratil in those years. Everybody called her Pepinka. She became a veritable anchor of love and support for Marie.

Marie's ties to her father were of a somewhat different nature. They vacillated—as she was to relate later in a collection of autobiographical sketches entitled *Meine Kinderjahre*

(My Childhood Years)—between love and fear. To quote from this work, which she wrote many years later in Rome at the age of seventy: "I knew quite well what fear was, for my sister and I had grown up in fear of dad. It was spoon-fed to us since early childhood by means of a threat which was never put into effect, yet was effective just the same: 'Just you wait. I'll tell your dad and then you'll see!'"[9]

A volatile type, given to sudden outbursts and emotional explosions, it was rather easy for him to instill awe in his children. The range of his emotions was, to say the least, amazing: "As pleasant as dad could be in times of calm, he would act awful when in one of his incomprehensible and easily induced states of anger" (190). Moreover, his occasionally uttered threats did not exactly endear him to his children. One of his favorite utterances was: "I don't want to be loved, just feared!" (191). Marie's younger half brothers were much less taken in by these threatening remarks, not incorrectly believing that much of his tough talk was just bluster. Much more serious than his blustering rhetoric was the fact that he took little interest in his children's education. As a result, a motley retinue of nursemaids, governesses, and tutors, to whom the children did not relate well, were brought into the house.

Not surprisingly, however, there were many redeeming features about Marie's father, which caused her relationship with him to be on the whole rather good. In the first place, although not an avowed liberal, he was tolerant toward people of other nationalities and faiths. This was especially noteworthy with regard to the French, whom he had met and fought in combat as mortal enemies. His views of them can be summarized in his statement: " . . . we shot and killed the enemy, but we did not slander him" (206). He was equally broad-minded in matters of faith but railed against the notion of communicating with the dead, regarding it to be stark superstition: "There is no path to us from beyond, otherwise my brothers would have found it" (204). Marie described her father's main virtues as a sense of justice, a lack of stubbornness, courage, and faithfulness to principle. His main weaknesses, according to her, were his anger and his bad temper All in all, he married four times. In 1825 he married the orphaned daughter of the highly acclaimed Baron von Sorgenthal. She died soon. His marriage to Marie's mother, whom he wed in 1829. was a true love match. After her passing away, he was so devastated that he contemplated suicide. But in due time he decided to marry for a third time. Death was to take his third wife as well. His fourth wife died when he was an old man. He followed her into death soon thereafter.

Pater Borek was the family priest in Zdislawitz. He tutored Marie and her older sister in religion. At the age of eight, Marie experimented with her own mortality by attempting to jump out of a window. Instead of turning into an angel, as she had hoped, her daring undertaking merely resulted in a big bump on her head and a mild scolding by the priest. Two years prior to this event, in 1836, a cholera epidemic struck the community. Both the priest and the young Jewish town physician, Dr. Engel, were busy saving lives. The latter "struggled for the poorest of his patients with the same care as for the wealthiest one" (254). He saved the life of one of Marie's brothers, Adolf. Her father could not praise Dr. Engel enough: "His name is not just 'Angel.' He is an angel" (256). In later years, he referred to both men with the highest possible praise: "Surely, the Jewish physician and the Catholic priest. All due respect: Both were heroes" (256).

From childhood on, Marie spent the summers and the warmer parts of spring and fall at Zdislawitz, her ancestral estate in Moravia. Not surprisingly, Zdislawitz and its surroundings were in later years to become the background of many of her literary works. During the cold season, she and her family stayed in the glittering capital city of Vienna. As was customary in those days, the wealthy Dubsky family had in addition to its permanent country residence in Moravia also acquired a stately apartment in a townhouse at the Haarmarkt. It was called the "Three Raven House." Marie established a strong bond with this place and returned to it for decades even after her marriage, until the building was razed toward the turn of the century to make way for new dwellings. While Zdislawitz provided her later with the topics and themes prevalent in her stories about the countryside and life in the village and manor, Vienna became the background of her literary endeavors dealing with city life and the aristocratic society there. This city was for her a fountainhead of accumulated knowledge, ready and eager to give to anyone willing to learn. From the very onset it was therefore more than merely the political center of the empire. The Burgtheater (Theater of the [Imperial] Castle), however—a place she truly worshiped—was the city's innermost intellectual and spiritual core. She looked at this classical theater as being both a temple and a provider of education.

The duality of personal background and attachment, Zdislawitz and Vienna, permeated her entire life and provided the foundation along intellectual and creative lines for her later career as a writer. The fairy tales which her Bohemian nurse told her in early childhood stimulated her imagination. Further stimulation was provided by the fairy-tale collection of the French writer Charles Perrault, which she practically devoured after she learned to read. Soon enough, Marie herself began to write in prose and verse. Having learned to master Czech and French early in life, she wrote in French long before she attempted to write in German. The explanation of this, to outsiders, perhaps peculiar circumstance is simple. Her protracted contacts as a child with nannies, servants, governesses, and tutors caused her to be emotionally and intellectually closer to Czech and French than to German.

When she was ten years old, her aunt Helene's grown son, Moritz von Ebner-Eschenbach, a military officer whom the children called "uncle," read by chance some of Marie's French poems. One of them was an ode praising Napoleon. He took an interest in her efforts and responded by sending her Zedlitz's *Loblied auf den Rhein* (Song of Praise to the Rhine) with the admonition to express herself in German in future writing attempts. Two years later, on June 21, 1842, her father provided her with her second stepmother, Xaverine Countess Kolowrat, a blonde and beautiful woman in her early thirties, whom he married in Vienna. Mama Xaverine, as she was soon called, her father's fourth wife, was highly educated, well read, and also artistically gifted. She was the one who opened the gate to German literature for Marie even further.

The main impulse, however, for becoming a writer of German came unwittingly from her father. He provided her with an experience that was to leave a deep and permanent imprint: her first visit to a theater. It was the Carl-Theater in Vienna—still called Kasperle-Theater (Punch Theater) in those years. In the nearby Theater an der Wien (Theater on the Vienna River), to which her father also took her, Ferdinand Raimund's *Mädchen aus der Feenwelt* (The Girl from the Fairy World) was playing. Raimund, popular with the theater-going public as a local playwright and a master of fairy plays and magic shows, was also her father's favorite dramatist. These first theater experiences stimulated Marie's interest in plays and caused her to devise dramatic plots of her own. Although she did not write them down at that time but related them to her sister and mutual friends, the children acted some of them out together. By that time Marie had turned twelve. From now on her father regularly took her to the theater while they stayed in Vienna in the winter months.

Her new "mother" gave her a one-volume collection of Schiller's dramas for her next birthday. She had occasion to see Schiller's dramas on the stage at the Burgtheater, the most renowned stage in Vienna, on which classical as well as contemporary dramatic masterpieces were performed. Little wonder then that this playwright soon became her favorite. At the Burgtheater she also saw Lessing's *Minna von Barnhelm* and Goethe's *Egmont*. In no time at all her enthusiasm for the theater knew no bounds. After some especially memorable visits to the Burgtheater, she felt that she was destined to become a dramatist herself:

> During many such solemn evenings I sat on the little bench in the rear of our box [in the theater]. My head was burning. My cheeks were glowing. One cold shower after the other went down my spine and I was thinking: in the not too distant future, your plays will shoot down from the stage like sparks. What a time! Every single hour affirmed my conviction that I was destined to become the Shakespeare of the nineteenth century. (*Aus meinen Kinder- und Lehrjahren*, 76-77).

These regular visits to the theater after her twelfth birthday were doubly beneficial for the growing teenager. In the first instance, Marie became very familiar with the stage and its possibilities. In addition, she also came to know contemporary and classical German and foreign dramatists and their best-known works. This continuing exposure stimulated her imagination even further, contributing not only to her enthusiasm for the theater, but also engendering the urge to develop the skill to fashion her own dramatic stories and plots. Soon enough, her growing enthusiasm extended to creative writing in general. On the eve of her fourteenth birthday, Marie wrote to a former governess, to whom she kept up a personal correspondence, that she wanted to become "the greatest woman writer of all nations and ages" or die (*Aus meinen Kinder- und Lehrjahren*, 77). Although the early results were rather meager, consisting of an epic dealing with personages in Roman history and a few poems, the incentive toward later achievements was there. Secondly, and just as importantly for her future development as a creative woman writer, she made increasing use of German as a vehicle of literary expression.

In the course of these early developmental and growth years, Marie's family had grown in number. Two step-brothers, with whom she also was to have close familial relations over the years, had been added. In 1843 her father had been honored by the emperor by being granted the title of count. Her "new" mother's gift of Schiller's works had made this dramatist not only her favorite poet and writer, but had also presented her with models and patterns begging to be imitated and emulated. Xaverine was well aware of the grow-ing infatuation on the part of her stepdaughter with literature and literary endeavors. She also observed Marie's vacillation between states of outwardly boyish wildness and defiance and a romantic inclination toward periods of nearly total withdrawal into a world of inner reality and dreams. But the obvious *Dichterdrang* (urge to become a writer) of young Marie was out of step with the mores of her aristocratic class. Members of the higher aristocracy, to which she belonged, simply did not aspire to become writers. This unwritten law was all the more observed if they were females. Her family, with the exception of "Uncle" Moritz, consequently frowned on her literary plans and ambitions. In 1847, when Marie turned seventeen, her second stepmother wanted to obtain, so to speak, an expert opinion about the level of Marie's literary talent. She turned for this purpose to Austria's premier writer, Franz Grillparzer, whom she knew and respected. "Mama" Xaverine sent samples of Marie's poems to Grillparzer with

the expectation that he would consider them so inferior that
Marie would be permanently healed of her attraction to writing. Deep inside, she might even have harbored the hope that
this former theater celebrity—now in self-imposed retirement
for nearly a decade—might pass a negative judgment on
Marie's writing as a matter of course. On reading Marie's
poetry, Grillparzer wanted to convey his impressions in person but found the countess not at home. In consequence, he
put his favorable remarks in writing, resulting in a letter to
the countess which, considering her negative frame of mind
in this matter, surprised her greatly. The letter reads in part:

> The poems show unmistakable traces of talent. A most
> fortunate ear for verse, the power of expression, a
> perhaps overly profound sentiment, insight, and a keen
> gift for judgment in many of her satirical poems form
> a talent which elicits interest. The neglect of its
> cultivation might hardly be in the power of its owner.
> What is still lacking is that maturity which transforms
> a poet into an artist, that pervasive lucidity which
> transfers the thought unimpeded on to the listener (or
> perhaps even the reader?).[10]

This letter, largely ignored by the family, became a source of
both comfort and inspiration for Marie in future years. Grillparzer's words of praise imbued her spirit with ever greater
determination to pursue a literary career. But this was not the
end of her personal attachment to Grillparzer. In future years
a close professional and personal relationship akin to a genuine friendship bound the maturing woman writer to the aging
and progressively more reclusive dramatist and Viennese
sage, as she richly documented in her second important book
of recollections, *Erinnerungen an Grillparzer* (Recollections
about Grillparzer). From her remarks we gather that the deep

respect, even adoration she felt for the master at the beginning of their association gradually grew into a close father-daughter relationship, filling to some extent the partial void that the uneven relations with her own father had left in her psyche. Earlier on, however, and on her own initiative, she sent some of her poems to Betty Paoli, a lyricist whose poetry was especially appreciated and even celebrated among women at that time. Betty Paoli's reply, although not as comforting as that of Grillparzer, encouraged Marie as well to continue her efforts to improve her skills as a writer, an aspiration which she was able to take very seriously in the next three decades. Her contact with this well-known contemporary woman writer was—similar to that with Grillparzer—to expand over the years into the higher sphere of intellectual and professional friendship.

Marie Dubsky's childhood unfolded in retrospect in a highly protected and protective environment. She was afforded a limited and a limiting change of scenery and social landscape, extending from the ancestral castle setting and adjacent village life in Moravia to the city dwelling and experience of city life in the social and cultural scene of Vienna. Because of social mores practiced among the high aristocracy, her personal contacts with her parents were, of course, also highly restricted. The constant flow of changing governesses and tutors—not to speak of her two stepmothers again —left feelings of void in the psyche of the maturing girl. What she perhaps missed the most was the knowledge and concomitant inner reassurance that come from constant and continually reinforced, and consequently deeply felt, parental love. There were, to be sure, other disappointments clouding the generally fair sky of her youth. Soon enough she and her siblings discovered that older people did not always keep their word. The children were, in effect, quite frequently subjected to falsehoods and lies by the people around them: "Didn't

people know any better than to lie to us and to deceive us?"
(*Meine Kinderjahre,* Hafis 12:314). The disappointments
arising from these negative experiences were also encountered in another area. In these days, Marie soon began to
doubt the words of the Bible regarding the stars and their
function: "No, no, not for that purpose! They were not just
created so that we could enjoy their view and find satisfaction in it. They were created for themselves and most of
them so much larger than our earth, just as it is much larger
than a speck of dust dancing in the sunlight" (*Meine Kinderjahre,* Hafis 12:314). At this stage in her development, she
also began to doubt her relationship with God: "Does my
voice get through to Him? Does He know about me" . . . My
thanks did not reach Him at all—He had no knowledge of
me" (*Meine Kinderjahre,* Hafis 12:314).

These were also the years during which Marie Dubsky's
interest in literature became a permanent as well as dominant
feature in her life. The event which was perhaps most crucial,
albeit painful, in bringing about this development was the
death of her beloved grandmother on her mother's side and
the inheritance of a large collection of books stemming from
her grandfather. Again Marie comments in her autobiographical essay: "With voracious appetite I devoured whatever
dramas were available to me, plays of Shakespeare, Racine,
Corneille, Goethe, Kleist, and I regretted only that my poor
grandmother did not have a single work of ancient literature
[in her collection], [writings] in which Lessing was immersed
when he was of my age" (*Meine Kinderjahre,* Hafis 12:343-
344). Delving into this rich cultural and intellectual legacy
also led Marie to reflect on herself and on her status as a
young woman in a man's world:

> The high opinion I had about my talent, my eagerness
> to learn, my thirst for knowledge suffered a strong

blow when I attempted [to draw] a comparison between myself and the child Gotthold Ephraim [Lessing]. . . . He studied even in his spare time in school, and ancient writers whose names I never even heard pronounced "were his world."

That is the world where children are made who are to become future greats—that is not how I was [made]. . . . It was a bitter time of introspection, filled with longing and sorrow, this very first time which I spent eye to eye with the inhabitants of my grandmother's bookcase. (*Meine Kinderjahre,* Hafis 12:342-343).

These observations, bitter as they are, culminate in a crescendo of self-doubt that reflects and documents her early conditioning in a male-oriented society which denied a woman equal access to schooling and education: "What would people think of me if I were to begin studying Greek or Latin? They would simply call me deranged. I was just a girl. The world was full of activities [which were] not considered to be proper and right for a girl: The walls rising around me, between which my writing and my endeavors were permitted to unfold, were sky-high. They fenced me in." (*Meine Kinderjahre,* Hafis 12:344).

Her inner turmoil, displaying also a goodly amount of pent-up anger at the social injustice she had to suffer, was soon to be accompanied by upheavals in the outside world. When Marie Dubsky reached the age of seventeen, Austria and the rest of Central Europe, taking the cues from the continent's perennial revolutionary hotbed, which was France, were on the verge of major civil unrest. 1847 was indeed a year of general unease in Austria. The prices for bread and meat had to be substantially raised, leading to civic defiance of the authorities and even violent acts on the part of the poorer population, which felt especially hard-pressed by the steep rise in the cost of living. At the height of the turmoil, unemployed workers plundered food stores in Vienna. A worker in those days earned barely fifty kreuzer a day. The annual income of a government official, on the other hand, consisted of the handsome average sum of 400 guilders. A few privileged individuals—not to speak of the earnings of the most favored members of society in those days, the aristocracy—fared substantially better. Gifted commoners, for example, could accumulate substantial wealth. A case in point is the famous and popular actor, director, and playwright in one, Johann Nepomuk Nestroy, who at the height of his popularity earned the phenomenal sum of 10,000 guilders.

The revolutionary year of 1848 led in time to some improvements in the lot of the average Austrian citizen, at least in the major cities of the country, but—viewed from the vantage point of the fledgling liberal movement of the age—it also resulted in worsening conditions in its immediate aftermath. At first, to be sure, the March revolution looked very promising. It brought freedom of the press after the collapse of the Metternich regime and its censorship. It also witnessed the founding of general workers' societies. Karl Marx came to Vienna and stayed for a while. But developments toward genuine democracy in the land were only temporary. Soon enough the conservative and reactionary forces within the Danube monarchy regained the upper hand. The subsequent October revolution can be compared to the powerful aftershocks of a deadly earthquake. It exploded in bloody street battles in Vienna and Prague and resulted in thousands of casualties, among whom at least 2,000 died. Although the overthrow of the repressive and ossified Metternich system, the forced abdication of the mentally deficient Emperor Leopold I, and the inauguration of his young successor to the Habsburg throne, who was to become Franz Joseph I of Austria, looked very promising at first, true liberalism and genuine movement toward more democratic institutions within the monarchy were slow in the making and still decades away. Temporary comfort was obtained only in the final freeing of the peasants throughout the realm, the culmination of a development which had already begun nearly a century earlier by direction of the enlightened Emperor Joseph II.[11]

The two decades between 1846 and 1866 were formidable ones for Austria in its continuous struggle to survive as a viable multinational empire. The venerable Habsburg monarchy was gravely threatened with disintegration from within and dismemberment from the outside. The monarchy's last brilliant statesman after Metternich's fall, Prince Felix zu Schwarzenberg—a man with strong conservative convictions, who was strongly dedicated to monarchical principles and to preserving Austrian hegemony in Central Europe and in the Balkans—tried in vain to stem the tide of history that eventually was to sweep the Danube monarchy away. Appointed as prime minister of Austria by the young and inexperienced Franz Joseph, he displayed extraordinary skills in preserving the political integrity and standing of the empire at a time when it was mortally threatened by multiple upheavals including a nationalist insurrection in Hungary. Moreover, he succeeded as well in checking, at least temporarily, the expansionist drive of Prussia while still in office. One can safely surmise that he would have been a more than adequate match for Bismarck's political maneuverings in the 1860s and early 1870s, had he not died prematurely in 1852.

The historically auspicious year of 1848 proved to be memorable and filled with excitement for Marie Dubsky not only on account of the political and social upheaval in the country. It was filled with excitement also along personal lines. In July of that year, Marie became the wife of her cousin Moritz von Ebner-Eschenbach, with whom she had enjoyed the friendliest of familial relations since childhood. He was her elder by fifteen years. Their marriage, by all accounts a most happy one, was to last fifty years to end only with his death in 1898. However, it remained childless. This highly educated and cultured imperial officer and teacher was unique in her family, in that he was the only one who, at least initially, supported and even encouraged her literary ambitions. A brief excursus on his life and career is important not only to provide the background of this brilliant man, but also to show his influence on his new wife. In the first decades of their long marriage, his career as a military officer, professor, and research scientist completely overshadowed the efforts of his young wife to embark on her own career as a writer.

Moritz was born on November 27, 1815, the son of a highly decorated military officer. His father, Nikolaus von Ebner-Eschenbach, was an offspring of an old Nuremberg patrician family, which became impoverished during the Napoleonic wars. He began his career as an apprentice in a glove-maker's shop and ended it after remarkable achievements as a lieutenant general, knight of the *Theresienorden* (Order of [the Empress] Maria Theresa), and co-director of the imperial corps of engineers. When Moritz reached the age of five, his father married Helene Baroness von Dubsky after his first wife, Moritz's natural mother, passed away. His stepmother Helene guided the boy's education. Since she had lost two brothers in the War of Liberation and saw her third brother Franz, Maria's future father, gravely wounded, she did not want Moritz to pursue a military career. She therefore insisted that he attend the *Theresianum*[12] in order to embark later in life on a career as a government official. But despite her wishes, Moritz decided on his own initiative to join the military and enrolled subsequently in the military engineering academy. It was obvious that he felt the overpowering urge to follow in his father's footsteps. At the age of eighteen he obtained his lieutenant's commission. At twenty-five, the serious-minded young officer—a student and a friend of the Viennese physicist Ettinghausen—became a professor of chemistry and physics at the engineering academy, by all accounts a remarkable achievement. Artistically talented as well, he played the piano in his spare time and even composed for it. Later in his life Moritz von Ebner-Eschenbach wrote a detailed autobiography, which was published posthumously in the *Münchner Allgemeine Zeitung* (Munich Daily) in 1899 under the title *Erinnerungen des k.u.k. Feldmarschalleutnants a.D. Moriz Freiherrn von Ebner-Eschenbach* (Recollections of the I[mperial] and R]oyal] Lieutenant General i[n] R[etirement] Moriz Baron von Ebner-Eschenbach).[13]

During his successful teaching career, which he pursued for eighteen years—first in Vienna and after the reestablishment of the academy in Klosterbruck near Znaim he trained many young officers. He traveled extensively as part of his calling, visiting Italy several times. He also journeyed to Dalmatia, Constantinople, Paris, and London. He even went as far as Egypt, when he attended the opening of the Suez Canal. In 1856, after he had advanced to the rank of major, he became head of the so-called *Geniekomitee* (Special Engineer Corps). All these advancements were the result of his excellent standing and reputation as a researcher and military scientist. The physicist/philosopher Ernst Mach[14] praised him for his contributions to Austrian technology. Ebner-Eschenbach pushed for the use of electrically detonated mines and constructed large searchlights which were used successfully in the defense of Venice in 1859. In this year he also succeeded in closing the harbor of Venice with sea mines of his own invention. When the Vienna city walls, which surrounded the inner city and hampered its expansion and modernization, were scheduled for razing, the baron was called upon for technical assistance. His mines brought down the ancient fortifications at the *Schottentor* (Gate of Scots) and the *Stubentor* (Gates of Stuben). His liberal views, on the other hand, led to his early retirement at the age of fifty-nine. In his calm, deliberate, and scholarly style he describes this event as follows: "[In 1874] I was ordered into retirement while simultaneously being advanced to the rank of lieutenant general, and I departed from military service after having dedicated thirty-eight years of my life to it."[15] On the positive side, though, his retired status permitted him to engage in even more extended travel than earlier. He was able to go as far abroad as Iceland and Persia. He also occupied his time in later years with extensive historic and philosophical studies until his death as an octogenarian in 1898.

Shortly after his marriage to Marie Dubsky, the young couple settled in Vienna, where the baron had professional and teaching commitments. It is noteworthy that certain parallel events in the lives of his young wife and the youthful Austrian Emperor Franz Joseph continued. In 1848 the latter also married. The beautiful, intelligent, and highly cultured Wittelsbach Princess Elisabeth became his bride, and the couple also settled in the capital city. However, another event was to be of much greater future impact on Marie von Ebner-Eschenbach's later life and development as a writer. 1848 was also the year of birth of Karl Emil Franzos, who was to become one of the most influential writers and publicists in the 1880s and 1890s and the editor and publisher of the prestigious literary periodical *Deutsche Dichtung* (German Literature). In this capacity he was able to be instrumental in helping to spread Marie von Ebner-Eschenbach's reputation as an author.[16]

All the while in this revolutionary year, the newly wedded couple sympathized with those circles of the Austrian nobility which were dissatisfied with the repressive measures of the Metternich system and could therefore be labeled as liberal and progressive. The Ebner-Eschenbachs, in effect, subscribed wholeheartedly to the ideas of such liberal political lyricists and writers as Anastasius Grün—in actuality a member of high nobility, whose given name was Count Anton Alexander von Auersperg—who propagated far--reaching reforms not only in the government, but also in the army and even in the church. Yet their stay in Vienna, also the center of political crosscurrents, was not to be of long duration. Fortunately for the future of the baron, his transfer was not at all related to his privately held political views. The military institute at which he taught was transferred to Klosterbruck near Znaim.

In 1850 the couple established itself in Louka, a small provincial town in the general vicinity of Klosterbruck. In this rustic environment, almost completely cut off from the rest of the world, Marie von Ebner-Eschenbach was to spend the next ten years of her life. That these years did not turn out to be a completely wasted time of stagnation and mental deterioration for her is an indication of the young woman's indomitable will to make the best of her life even under the most unfavorable circumstances and to grow intellectually, no matter the obstacles. In one of her last novellas, *Das Schädliche* (The Pernicious), written decades later, she conveys impressions and recollections from the many reclusive days she spent in Louka. She was determined at the time to engage in extensive studies there and to turn a seeming debacle into a superb period of learning and growth. An early riser, she embarked on autodidactic studies, thereby amassing and intellectually incorporating a substantial knowledge of history as well as other areas of immediate interest to her. All along, she worked to improve her mastery of German syntax and her understanding of a broad spectrum of interrelated subjects, such as prosody, logic, aesthetics, and literature in general. In Joseph von Weilen, a colleague of her husband who also taught at the academy and who was to make himself a name as a dramatist as well as an adviser to the cultured and politically astute Austrian Crown Prince Rudolf,[17] she found a friend and a like-minded intellectual partner. Not only did he stimulate and further nurture her love for the theater. He also gave her invaluable advice regarding the craft of writing.

While Marie Ebner, as she began to call herself, embarked on pursuing her intellectual and literary interests in the first decade of her marriage, her husband Moritz was able to advance his career as a military scientist. As a result of his treatise, *Über die Anwendung der Reibungs-Elektrizität zum Zünden von Sprengladungen* (About the Use of Frictional Electricity for [the purpose of] Igniting Explosive Charges), he was asked to give up his teaching post in the provincial academy and to join the *Geniekomitee* in Vienna as a major.

In 1858 *Aus Franzensbad: Sechs Episteln von keinem Propheten* (From Franzensbad: Six Epistles by No Prophet), Marie Ebner's first literary work—a satire about a woman's adventures on her way to a spa and while staying there—was published anonymously in Leipzig. By no means a masterpiece it nonetheless gave a hint of a special gift of tongue-in-cheek humor, which the authoress was to develop years later and interweave with the strands of many of her future stories. Decades later she wrote about this work in a special edition of *Deutsche Dichtung,* giving her contribution a strong infusion of autobiographical detail. In this omnibus volume, entitled *Mein Erstlingswerk* (My First Piece of Writing), she was to share the honor of writing about first literary endeavors with such contemporary literary luminaries as Theodor Fontane, Conrad Ferdinand Meyer, Gustav Freytag, Paul Heyse,[18] and Karl Emil Franzos, who was also the volume's editor and publisher. Just as noteworthy is the fact that she was the only woman writer among the contributors to the common effort.

In the same year in which *Sechs Episteln* was first published, Moritz Ebner was entrusted with the task off demolishing the old city walls of Vienna. Two years later, the couple moved to the capital city on a permanent basis. They lived in the old house on the Rotenturmstrasse, which Marie's family had chosen as their winter residence in past years. As in her youth, Marie Ebner spent the winters there. During the warm season in spring and in the summer she preferred the solitude and the scenic beauty of St. Gilgen at the Wolfgangsee (Lake Wolfgang), in the fall she stayed quite often at the old estate of Zdislawitz, which was managed by one of her brothers.

But this idyllic lifestyle was misleading. Marie Ebner's youthful ambition to be a female Shakespeare, nurtured now for over fifteen years, continued to reverberate in her soul. Deep within, she wanted to be more than the cultured wife of a famous military scientist. Nor did she obtain any special satisfaction from her aristocratic background that afforded her entry into the highest aristocratic circles. Fortunately for her, as in past decades, her husband was still supportive of her aims and did not discourage her at first in her ongoing literary pursuits. In 1860 the time of arrival and recognition by the public seemed to be at hand. This was the year in which she completed her first historical tragedy. The play, *Maria Stuart in Schottland* (Mary Stuart in Scotland), was conceived as a dramatic introduction and prelude to Schiller's earlier drama *Maria Stuart*. It was meant to present the historic events in Scotland preparing and leading up to Mary

Stuart's dramatic confrontation with Queen Elizabeth and her subsequent execution in England by the queen's order. The well-known theater impresario Eduard Devrient[19] presented this *Schauspiel in fünf Aufzügen* (Drama in Five Acts), the author of which gave her name as M. von Eschenbach. in Karlsruhe. It found a favorable reception there. Devrient himself was so impressed with this drama—which was written in the manner of German Classical style in iambic meter—that he proposed it for the Schiller prize. Although the play failed to be honored in this way and was severely criticized by the well respected German writer and dramatist Otto Ludwig—who took its author "M. v. Eschenbach" to be a man—Marie Ebner was beside herself with joy and pride.

This first success of one of her plays was followed by a second, which looked nearly as spectacular at the outset. Two years later, in 1862, her one-act play, *Die Veilchen* (The Violets), was performed in the Vienna Burgtheater. Was this the breakthrough she had dreamed about in all these many years? At last this famous stage had opened its gates to her. Regrettably, however, this event—as emotionally uplifting as it was to her—proved to be only short-lived. It did not lead to the hoped-for breakthrough that would have ensured her of a permanent public recognition of her talent as a dramatist. Of greater future value to her was the beginning in 1863 of a life-long friendship with Ida von Fleischl-Marxow, one of the most brilliant Viennese women of the period. This intellectually versatile woman read all of Marie von Ebner-Eschenbach's manuscripts in subsequent years in a supportive, yet still critical manner and became her literary adviser and guide.

The year 1867—politically significant because of the Austro-Hungarian *Ausgleich* (accommodation), which divided the empire into two autonomous halves by creating two independent parliaments—led to the establishment of another enduring literary friendship in Marie von Ebner-Eschenbach's life. She met and befriended the gifted writer Ferdinand von Saar, whose melancholy novellas focused on the timely theme of decadence in Austrian Society.[20] The next year, 1868, brought some liberalization of political and social conditions in Vienna as well, notably the official tolerance of public gatherings of workers demonstrating for the right to establish unions. In addition a restructuring of the criminal code along more humanitarian lines led to the discontinuance of public executions. That year, in fact, witnessed the very last public execution in the empire. On the negative side, however, Czech nationalists staged protracted political protests which resulted in violence. They questioned the legality of the imperial *Reichsrat* (Imperial Council) to represent their national concerns and demanded full Czech autonomy on an equal footing with that which the Hungarians had already achieved. As a result of the unrest, martial law was declared in the crownland of Bohemia.

Twenty years after the continent-wide upheavals of 1848, the political and social atmosphere of Europe was charged with revolutionary fervor again. In this for Marie Ebner important year of 1868, her second full-fledged tragedy, *Marie Roland,* a play about the French revolution of 1789, was performed in Weimar. The drama, also written in the Classical style of her first tragedy, could not be shown in Vienna because of the constraints put on it by Austria's still active censors. The former "Young German" author Heinrich Laube,[21] now director of the Vienna Burgtheater, pleaded in vain to the Austrian authorities to permit the showing of the play. The censors met his argument, that Madame Roland portrayed a nonviolent individual representing the moderate wing of the Parisian political spectrum at the time of the French Revolution, with a counterargument of their own. They contended that the drama reflected the poisoned atmosphere of the period much too faithfully to be viewed by the public. Even Eduard Devrient, who had the highest regard for Marie Ebner's talent as a dramatist and had proved it by showing her *Maria Stuart in Schottland* at the court theater in Karlsruhe for several performances, lacked the courage to stage her politically controversial *Marie Roland* there. The brief showing of the play in Weimar, one of Europe's most liberal locales, had therefore little impact on its further fate on the stage, which—as the future was to demonstrate—was doomed from the outset.

The immediate consequences of this failure for the further development of Marie Ebner as an aspiring woman dramatist were of major proportions. Not only did it deal a devastating blow to her expectations and her pride as an author. She was also stamped a literary radical by the board of censors, and a woman at that. All further attempts on her part to ensure for herself a foothold on the stage were equally thwarted. To be sure, in 1869 her one-act play *Doktor Ritter,* her second drama beholden to Schiller, was performed a few times at the Burgtheater. Its historic action, dramatizing Schiller's brief stay in Bauerbach after fleeing the confinement of Stuttgart and also his unrequited love for Lotte Wollzogen, failed to capture the public's fancy. After the failure of her comedy *Das Waldfräulein* (The Young Lady of the Forest), which Laube staged at the Vienna Stadttheater (City Theater) in 1873, the deeply hurt and saddened Marie Ebner stopped writing for the stage altogether. The newspapers had criticized her play and her skills as a playwright too severely. Her husband became concerned. His good name and the family honor were besmirched. By withdrawing from the theater, his wife's earliest and most profound love and ambition as a writer, she was in the best company, following in the footsteps of her fatherly friend and mentor Franz Grillparzer.[22] Yet in contrast to the latter, who had continued writing dramas even after forsaking the stage, Marie Ebner's trauma proved so severe that, with the exception of a few experimental *Dramolets* (short dramatic sketches), she wrote no further plays in future years, not even—as did Grillparzer—for the proverbial desk drawer.

Should this obvious failure and seeming disgrace cause Marie Ebner to end her love affair with literature altogether, a calling which apparently was stymied in its infancy? While she struggled with the answer to this fateful question, her husband's chosen career was going in the opposite direction. The much respected engineer and scientist garnered additional acclaim in military circles with the publication of his forward-looking treatise *Der Luftballon und seine Anwendung im Kriege* (The Air Balloon and Its Use in War) in 1871. But in spite of giving in to feelings of jealousy and inferiority, Marie Ebner, unwilling to forsake her love for literature and her earlier dreams of contributing to it significantly someday, changed the direction of her literary endeavors. Much like Gottfried Keller and Conrad Ferdinand Meyer, who had also experienced insurmountable difficulties in their ambitious drives to become dramatists, she began to concentrate her literary skills on writing prose and on crafting narratives. Her consistent efforts in these directions soon expanded to open up new avenues of learning and growth for her. In 1875 she initiated first contacts with Julius Rodenberg, the influential editor and publisher of the leading literary journal *Deutsche Rundschau* (German Perspective). In the same year she met Gottfried Keller, who, even though not generally overly fond of women, recognized a kindred spirit in her and was from then on very favorably disposed toward her. She read the works of the successful German woman writer Annette von Droste-Hülshoff and began an intimate correspondence, extended over many years, with the—at the time—prominent Louise von François, whose novel in two volumes, *Die letzte*

Reckenburgerin (The Last Female Member of the Reckenburgs), published in 1871, is still recognized today as a valuable contribution to the literature of the age. The novella *Der arme Spielmann* (The Poor Musician), which her old friend and supporter Grillparzer had written, left an equally strong impression in her perceptive mind. However, not only German, but also foreign narrative authors exerted an impact on her during these transitional formative years. Foremost among them was the Russian realist Turgenev, who also influenced Franzos's narrative skills. Marie Ebner felt very close to Turgenev because they shared similar social origins. He was also of aristocratic background and came from a country environment. She admired the great intensity of his feelings and especially devoured his internationally highly acclaimed work *Zapiski ochotnika* (1852), which she read in its German version with the title *Aus dem Tagebuch eines Jägers* (From the Diary of a Hunter). In these *Hunter's Notes* she found everyday experiences from the lives of wealthy and cruel landowners and their hapless victims, the poor and exploited peasants, artfully sketched against a background of masterfully depicted nature scenes.

Marie Ebner's actual beginnings as a narrator can be traced back—if one discounts her immature satirical sketch *Aus Franzensbad*—to the year 1872, in which she wrote a full-fledged satire with tragic undertones in the garb of a fairy tale entitled *Die Prinzessin von Banalien* (The Princess of Banalia). A trip to Switzerland in the following year provided her with enough inspiration to conclude a first small volume of stories, which she simply called *Erzählungen* (Tales). It appeared in print in 1875 under the Cotta imprint. The most notable selection in it is *Der Spätgeborene* (The One Born Late), which relates the story of an artist. Here the author made the disappointments and anguish of her own formative years as a writer into the central theme. A year later, in 1876—she was forty-six now—the first true break-through occurred in her literary career. *Božena,* her first novel, was printed by the same publisher. The heroine in this narrative, which Marie Ebner began writing in 1875, is a Czech maid who serves her employer faithfully through three generations. This humble Slavic woman overcomes all of the difficulties that life imposes on her, including insult and injustice, not through rebellion but by quietly and lovingly suffering personal pain. Her willingness to sacrifice her own happiness for the sake of the well-being of those whom she serves lifts her nearly to the level of a saint.

In the same year of 1876, Marie Ebner wrote and com-pleted *Margarete,* a story which was to be published fifteen years later in 1891. Here she moved from the rural and manor-house background of her earlier tales to the frequently seedy world of high-living society types in Vienna. With *Die Freiherren von Gemperlein* (The Barons of Gemperlein),pub-lished in 1879 in the periodical *Die Dioskuren* (The Dioscu-ri), she convincingly enlisted the realm of humor. This comi-cal story of two bachelors from old-Austrian aristocratic stock who prove incapable of continuing their lineage also borders on the tragic. In their younger years they failed to find and marry the kinds of brides which their whimsical imagination had conjured up. Now in their old age, the passion to marry flares up once more in them. As it turns out, not only do they fall in love with the same woman, but their infatuation is also directed at one who has been happily married for years. While working on this partly humorous, partly melodramatic story, Marie Ebner wrote in her dairy: "I spent the day in the company of the 'Gemperlein Brothers.' The 'Barons' did not leave me for a moment. They were walking before me. They were talking. I didn't write. I copied." Evidently, her early schooling as a dramatist was now paying healthy dividends in her successful attempts at writing narrative prose.

But Marie von Ebner-Eschenbach did not perfect and hone her writing skills in order to be only a writer of fiction, interested in developing themes of love and devotion or to present life in the country, the village, the manor, and—by way of contrast—also in the city. In 1880 she published a volume of highly intellectual aphorisms which revealed her keen insights into the makeup of the human psyche and into the challenges of life in general. However, at the time it was not this volume that was to bring her public acclaim. The reading public of the 1880s took little notice of a woman writer who also had an extraordinary intellect. *Lotti, die Uhr-macherin* (Lotti, the Clock Maker), a work of fiction published in 1881 in the *Deutsche Rundschau,* finally led to the hoped-for miracle of public recognition of Marie Ebner's authorial skills and launched her eventual fame as a writer. After many decades of struggle, she had finally begun to approach the goal of her dreams and efforts. The pages of leading German periodicals opened themselves now to the woman author as she entered her sixth decade of life. As if by divine intervention, her name suddenly shone next to those of the most prominent German-speaking writers of the age: Keller, Heyse, Storm. Marie Ebner would forever be grateful to Julius Rodenberg, the magazine's publisher. She would in future decades also dedicate her—as it turned out—last successful book to him. Yet, as fact is proverbially at times stranger than fiction, still stranger quite frequently than both is the mood and fickleness of public opinion, leading to fame and fortune of some, the downfall and misfortune of others in the public eye. In spite of its popularity at the time, the overly sentimental story of Lotti, an industrious female artisan of lower bourgeois background who had to work for a living, is not acknowledged to be one of Ebner-Eschenbach's best works today. Lotti's resolve to sacrifice her hard-earned fortune for the benefit of her former fiancé leaves the modern reader somewhat bewildered, if not outright disapproving, rather than tearfully sympathetic, for—intentionally or not—her former lover is presented as a self-centered and selfish type, unworthy of such largesse and personal sacrifice. The example of unselfish and almost saintly behavior on the part of the female protagonist lacks the ring of authenticity. But to the reading public of the 1880s it seemed to provide a welcome antithesis to the writings of Paul Heyse—one of the most popular authors of the period[23]—who shows his heroes and heroines in the throes of self-immolating passion. Marie Ebner, on the other hand, portrays her protagonists quite often at the lofty moment of self-conquest, in the Classical manner of Schiller's Maria Stuart or Goethe's Iphigenie, differing only in her down-to-earth and modernistic social settings and style.

The newly found popularity of Marie Ebner's writings opened the door for introducing also some of her earlier narratives to the reading public at large. The collection *Neue Erzählungen* (New Tales, 1881) reflected an initial attempt to satisfy the reading public's interest in her literary output. Two years later, in 1883, a second collection of stories, entitled *Dorf- und Schlossgeschichten* (Stories from the Village and the Castle) appeared. It contained three novellas that were to become perennial favorites among readers: *Der Kreisphysikus* (The District Physician), *Jakob Szela,* and, above all, the most famous animal story in German literature, *Krambambuli,* which is still widely read in schools throughout the German-speaking countries and therefore known to practically every youngster there. Much less publicized is the fact that this dramatic story of the life and death of a dog torn in his attachment and fidelity between two masters is very much indebted to Turgenev, whose earlier animal tales *Mumu* and *Komets Chertopkhanova*—the German title of which is *Tschertapchanows Ende* (Chertapkhanov's End)—influenced Marie Ebner greatly. The name "Krambambuli," however, appears to have been totally a product of her own poetic imagination.

Der Kreisphysikus and *Jakob Szela* are historical narratives which take the reader to the Austrian crownland of Galicia. In the conception of both tales Marie Ebner treats a region with which she had not dealt before as a writer. Yet despite the fact that she portrays a landscape and people that were quite different from those to which she was accustomed in her native Moravia and in Vienna, the novellas have the ring of authenticity. To be sure, as on previous occasions necessitating such intellectual preparation, she had read extensively about this unfamiliar environment. The Galician revolution of 1846 provides the historic setting in both tales. When Poland experienced its first territorial division among the imperial powers of Austria, Prussia, and Russia in 1772, Galicia became part of Austria. The province was geographically and ethnically divided into an eastern and a western part. While the east was primarily inhabited by Ukrainian peasants with a thin overlay of Polish nobility who owned most of the land, the western part had principally a Polish population. In both areas, yet preponderately so in the east, there was a large minority of Jews who had begun to settle there in the middle ages, speaking a language of their own, Yiddish, which had its roots in medieval German-Frankish dialects.[24] The revolution of 1846 in these parts is generally thought of as having been brought about by a drive of Polish nationalists to regain their national independence. Earlier such drives to free themselves from subjugation by Austria, Prussia, and Russia and to reestablish an independent Polish national state had been unsuccessful. The Galician uprising of 1846 also failed. Contributing factors for the regional unrest, however, were of a social nature. These undercurrents, in fact, especially prevalent among the peasantry, led to political tensions as well. In the novella *Der Kreisphysikus,* Marie Ebner describes these problems. Yet the narrative focuses primarily on the story's protagonist, the Jewish physician Rosenzweig, whose function as the regional doctor gives the novella its title. The plot of *Jakob Szela* makes it even clearer that the author, who for over a year had studied the history of the Galician uprising of 1846, was firmly convinced that the revolution resulted mainly from the social misery of the peasants.

In the next two stories, appearing in 1885, Marie Ebner changes her tone altogether. She leaves the area of politics and that of social and ethnic strife to return, at least in part, to a format she had employed earlier: humor and satire. The focus of these stories, collectively referred to as *Zwei Komtessen* (Two [Junior] Countesses), and their disclosure about the life of young women of noble birth immediately caught the public eye, increasing her popularity as a writer still further. The first of these two tales, *Komtesse Muschi*—a satirical portrait and sketch of an aristocratic teenager on the threshold of womanhood—is a monologue in letter form. It provides the reader with an inside glimpse into the intellectual and spiritual shallowness as well as into the boredom in the life of a young countess in the country. The second story, *Komtesse Paula,* is also a portrait of a young aristocratic protagonist, who relates her experiences and the story of her love in form of a diary. A much more sensible and intelligent young woman than Countess Muschi, who is immature and superficial, Countess Paula also writes in a more mature style. The language she employs and the views she expresses are consequently more reflective of her noble origins. The modern reader can readily sense and appreciate the autobiographical features in both works, in which the author presents the Goethean "two souls" in her own persona.

The stimulation of their success enabled her to produce a flood of published stories—some of shorter, some of longer format. The literary talent of this woman. nearing her sixtieth year of life, reached full bloom. Following the prose collection *Neue Dorf- und Schlossgeschichten* (New Stories from the Village and the Castle, 1886), the most notable tale of which is perhaps *Er lasst die Hand küssen* (He Sends a Hand Kiss)—a condemnation of the practice of cruel aristocrats of exerting nearly absolute control over the life and death of their dependent subjects, still observed in Austrian lands well into the nineteenth century—Marie Ebner published her most mature work of social consciousness, the novel *Das Gemeindekind* (The Ward of the Parish, 1887). In this developmental novel she expresses her faith in the capacity of the individual to overcome all obstacles of unfavorable heredity and environment provided that the individual gives free rein to the inner forces of good will and determination. In nearly total opposition to the doctrines of literary Naturalism, which was coming into vogue in Germany, she does not see man as a creature determined by external and internal forces beyond his control but rather the agent of his own fate through the power of free will.

Two more books were published in 1889. The first of these, which she called *Miterlebtes* (First-hand Experiences), draws heavily on her own experiences. The other, a frame story entitled *Ein kleiner Roman* (A Short Novel), alludes to the class conflict within Austrian society. The idealistic governess and tutor Helene and her pupil Anka personify the opposing and antagonistic societal forces in the land. This nationwide, sociopolitical antithesis between intellectually gifted members of the bourgeoisie and insensitive, ignorant representatives of the ruling aristocracy is reflected in *Ein kleiner Roman* in the relationship between Helene—a bright and sensitive woman eager to do what is right and good— and

Anka, the young and self-centered daughter of a count. Anka is both superficial and incapable of loving kindness. Her aristocratic father, although deeply in love with Helene, ultimately breaks with her to side with the whimsical and neurotic representative of the declining social class of which he is a member. Helene, on the other hand—though in her role as misunderstood, exploited, and spurned woman essentially a tragic figure—portrays the basically decent intentions and unspent psychic strength of the rising middle class. This inner theme of the narrative, reflected at the time in social and political developments in Austria-Hungary, reached even into the highest levels of society. For well over a decade a somewhat parallel struggle had taken place between the conservative emperor and his progressive and forward-looking son, Crown Prince Rudolf, who had embraced liberal and bourgeois values. Although largely hidden from public view and scrutiny, this struggle had tragic consequences for all. The highly gifted heir to the Habsburg throne, continually frustrated in his political plans for a liberalized and more democratic monarchy that was fully aware of and committed to the need of helping to overcome the cultural backwardness of Eastern Europe, committed suicide with his secret lover, Baroness Vetsera, in the imperial hunting retreat Meierling, south of Vienna, in the same year in which *Ein kleiner Roman* was published.[25] In previous years he had sensed that grave danger for the future viability of the Austro-Hungarian empire would arise in the Balkans and had prevailed on Karl Emil Franzos, who because of his earlier training as a journalist and his previous activities in these parts was an expert on Eastern European affairs, to do an investigative report for him on Serbia.

The politically cataclysmic suicide, boding ill for Austria's and for Europe's stability, if not development, left traces of deep concern and sorrow in Marie Ebner's psyche.

She had put a great amount of hope in the crown prince, whom she greatly admired and whose ideas of liberalization, she sensed, were needed to generate policies that were to ensure the survival of the monarchy to which she was viscerally attached. His tragic demise with its many political ramifications cast dark clouds over Austria's future. It was followed by a development in neighboring Germany in the subsequent year that was also to have far-reaching negative political consequences. The young, ambitious, and brash German Emperor Wilhelm II forced into retirement the aging, but doubtless cunning and wise chancellor Otto von Bismarck, who predicted in an uncanny fashion that any kind of trouble in the Balkans, the eastern powder keg of Europe, could start a devastating war.

As if these unfolding events were not enough of a shock, Marie Ebner's health began to deteriorate. In the tragic year of 1889 her psyche was struck by another devastating blow. She found out that she was suffering from an enlargement of the thyroid gland, an illness diagnosed as exophthalmic goiter. Although this malady was not life-threatening and could be controlled with medication, it resulted in a large and unsightly swelling of her neck which adversely affected her hitherto good looks. This disfiguring growth could not be covered up and hidden, not even by the then fashionable high-collar dresses. But not given to vanity as she had also not succumbed to vaingloriousness in the past, she resolved to continue with her life and her writing.

The year 1890 introduced Marie Ebner's fourth novel to the public. Neglected at first, perhaps because of its arcane title *Unsühnbar* (Inexpiatory), it can be regarded today as one of her most significant works, commenting, as it does, on the political and social developments of the entire epoch in an almost prophetic manner. Moreover, the author succeeded in creating a social novel of timeless import. She erected, in fact, the artful edifice of her fiction on an event that had actually taken place in the highest circles of contemporary Austrian aristocracy. But the plight of the story's heroine can still kindle our empathy today.

In all these years of writing and publishing her stories of love, intrigue, and high adventure, her personal life was rather quiet, sedate, and—her recent illness notwithstanding—devoid of outer excitement. To call it uneventful, however, would be incorrect. As her own career as a writer entered a number of phases to go eventually into high gear and to continue its frantic acceleration toward ever greater public and professional recognition, her husband's career—again by way of a reverse pattern—ended abruptly in retirement. We know from her diaries that her daily life was to a large extent routine, yet she never complained about it. Aside from being on a rather strict regimen—especially with regard to her creative writing—she engaged in active correspondence with friends and acquaintances and was also socially active in the close circle of her family and her friends. The high adventure and excitement that she craved, not least to find balance within herself, she experienced vicariously in the multiple and, at times, psychologically complex characters of her fiction.

That she may have had psychological problems of her own, however—not at all unusual in women of her status in Austrian society in that period—can be surmised from her association of long standing with Dr. Josef Breuer, with whom she kept up an active correspondence for decades.[26] Whereas there is little documentary evidence that Marie von Ebner-Eschenbach experienced severe marital problems and that her long-time marriage with her older cousin was not completely happy, the fact that her marriage was not blessed with children—for reasons which were never openly explained—must have left her unfulfilled in view of her boundless love of children, readily gleaned and richly documented in her fiction. Even such remarks of hers as: "A magnificent miracle happens to me through love, your love. The childless woman has the most children"—made late in her life—cannot completely disguise the fact that such a lack of offspring must have created and left a void in her, capable of causing psychological traumas. This void and the problems associated with it are definitely reflected in some of the female protagonists of her fiction. In the next three chapters of my study, I will have ample opportunity to demonstrate and document these reflections of inner personal turmoil.

In 1891, two of her other stories of unhappy love, *Margarete* and *Ohne Liebe* (Without Love), were published. These publications were followed in 1892 by a volume of three collected stories entitled *Drei Novellen* (Three Novellas). In *Oversberg, the* most outstanding narrative of the collection, the authoress succeeded in writing an acknowledged stylistic masterpiece, in which she makes the impossible appear feasible and gives a nearly perfect *Mustermenschen* (model human) the appearance of being not only pleasant but downright likable. A further jewel of Marie Ebner's narrative artfulness is *Glaubenslos?* (Without Faith?), which work she was able to publish in the following year. The well-known Grillparzer expert and contemporary Germanist August Sauer called it "her most profound and most significant novella about village life."[27] Be this as it may, the story—characterized as a *Dorfgeschichte* (tale about village life), in that it deals with contemporary life in an Austrian village—is a superb example of the flourishing *Heimatliteratur*[28] of the period. It appears to have been thematically influenced by Ludwig Anzengruber's dramas and novels.[29]

In the next three years, from 1894 to 1896, Marie Ebner witnessed the publication of four of her narratives: *Das Schädliche, Die Totenwacht* (The Death Watch), *Rittmeister*

Brand ([Cavalry] Captain Brand), and *Bertram Vogelweid.* These stories reflect the whole breadth of her narrative skills as well as her thematic range. They extend from serious to humorous subject matters and deal with life and people in the city as well as in the villages and countryside of her native Moravia. She also does not shy away in these tales from engaging her pen in occasional didacticism or social commentary. Thus, in the tragic novella *Das Schädliche,* she posits respect as the basis for all human interaction and as the bedrock of all attempts to raise and teach young people properly. In the course of the action, a father gives fate free rein when it threatens to destroy his heartless and insensitive daughter, in order that nature might rid itself of "the noxious thing"— as area hunters traditionally call a harmful animal. The authoress also counterposes all-pervasive love—the power of which as a driving force in human service or sacrifice for others she celebrates so frequently in most of her narratives—to the state of heartlessness and lack of basic human compassion. In the latter, she sees an indicator of isolationism and asocial behavior on the part of the individual. T h e element of humor and mild social criticism is preponderant in *Bertram Vogelweid.* Combining tongue-in-cheek humor, whim, wittiness, irony, and exuberance, the plot focuses on the fame and fortune of the journalist and writer Vogelweid, an overworked, highly nervous victim of the pressures of modern life, who yearns for the peace and quiet as well as the anticipated relaxation that a vacation in the country should provide. Marie Ebner gives a well executed parody of the harried writer, editor, and publisher Karl Emil Franzos, with whom she was well acquainted. As fate will have it, though, while staying at the castle of an aristocratic friend, Vogelweid unwittingly enters a den of literary dilettantes who make him a hapless victim of his journalistic fame. The plot allows the author to polemicize against the excesses of con-

temporary intellectual and political currents. Thus she attacks
Nietzscheanism as well as the nationalistic Young Czech
movement, Naturalism, and societal decadence.

Am Ende (At the End) and *Alte Schule* (Old School), two
collections of Marie Ebner's reflective and contemplative
writings, were published in 1897. They project in their titles
and contents thoughts of imminent death. But the sixty-
seven-year-old writer was not yet fated to die. Death and personal tragedy were nonetheless to affect her and her country
in the following year. On January 28, 1898, her husband
Moritz died in Vienna just before preparations could be final-
ized to celebrate their golden anniversary. Their longlasting
marriage and the happiness and harmony they achieved in it
can best be summarized by one of Marie Ebner's own aphorisms: "If the husband has the authority and the wife has the
brains, a good marriage results."[30]

In the same year 1898, the uncanny parallelism in the
lives of Marie von Ebner-Eschenbach and Emperor Franz
Joseph continued. Barely eight months after her husband's
death, a tragic happening struck the imperial household, sad-
dening the entire nation. Empress Elisabeth of Austria—
Franz Joseph's wife of fifty years, who ever since the suicide
of her son had traveled extensively and had spent a great deal
of her time away from the Vienna court at the Miramar castle
on the Adriatic Sea—was assassinated in Geneva on September 10, 1898, by the Italian anarchist Luigi Luccheni. In all
these years the Danube monarchy was also beset by a series
of government crises, which were shaking the state to its
very foundations. Political maneuvers were meant to save the
day. As a result, a number of emergency measures were
hastily instituted to hold together the venerable, but crum-
bling edifice of the multi-ethnic state by ever more desperate
means.

For the first time now, the widowed Marie von Ebner-

Eschenbach left her familiar surroundings in October of the same year for an extended stay abroad. She went to Italy and settled in Rome. But tragedy was to follow her there. She suffered a new shock in the following year, when word reached her that Ida von Fleischl-Marxow, her best friend, confidante, and adviser for decades, had passed away. In April 1899, she returned to Vienna, saddened beyond measure. Yet there was a turning point in the making there, which was about to result in happier days for her in the near future. Not so coincidentally, the happier days had a great deal to do with the approach of the new century. A number of high honors and festive occasions awaited her in the subsequent year in connection with the internationally celebrated turn of the century and the celebrations accompanying her seventieth birthday. In a special ceremony she became the first woman ever to receive an honorary doctorate from the venerable University of Vienna, the second-oldest university in the German-speaking world.[31] Her festive installation was accompanied by social and professional recognition of the highest order. Gerhart Hauptmann, Paul Heyse, Ferdinand von Saar, and Viktor Adler[32] were among the many literary and non-literary celebrities who paid homage to her as the "grösste Dichterin" (greatest woman writer) of the German-speaking world.

This unprecedented feting of a woman author in Austria's capital city was enthusiastically welcomed and publicly celebrated by the evolving indigenous feminist movement. Marie Ebner was presented with a written laudation signed by 10,000 Viennese women of all segments of society, adorned and artistically enhanced by women artists from the *Kunstschule für Frauen und Mädchen* (Art School for Women and Girls). Such public display of love and admiration was no coincidence, however. Marie Ebner had been interested in and supportive of feminine causes for many years. Ever since its founding in 1885, she had been a member in the *Verein der Schriftstellerinnen und Künstlerinnen in Wien* (Association of Women Writers and Artists in Vienna). This organization was comprised of women authors, artists, and musicians whose interests and financial security it was aiming to further. Marie Ebner served on the board of this association for many years and also contributed generously to its pension fund for needy members. By way of showing their appreciation, the club's members elected her as honorary member in the festive year of 1900.[33]

Nearly miraculously, her creative powers continued to flow unabated. Under the title of *Aus Spätherbsttagen* (From the Days of Late Autumn), a number of short stories and novellas were introduced to the reading public in 1901. Among them is *Die Spitzin* (The Female Pomeranian Dog), her second dramatic and heartrending animal tale. The story about the love and devotion of a female dog that is willing to give her life for her young provides one of the most sensitive interpretations of the psyche of an animal in world literature. *Der Vorzugsschüler* (The Honor Student), another memorable story, tells of an intellectually not overly gifted boy, whose tyrannical father drives him into suicide by overtaxing his capacity to learn and to succeed in school. The theme and its literary treatment confirm Marie Ebner's belief in an old pedagogical principle. The intellectual growth of a young person cannot be forced beyond its natural limitations without doing harm. Any attempt—especially if it is forceful—to push the parameters of the education of our youth beyond reasonable expectations is not only fated to be unsuccessful, but can also lead to tragic results. Both parents and teachers share the burden of responsibility.

Aged but intellectually unbroken, Ebner continued to write. She justifies this activity in one of her aphorisms: "Getting to be old means getting to be visionary" (*Aphoris-*

men, 66). In 1903 her narrative *Agave* was printed, and two years later a collection of novellas entitled *Die unbesiegbare Macht* (The Invincible Power). All were written from the vantage point of someone who had penetrated many of the mysteries of life. Education also plays an important role in these gems of wisdom. In *Agave* she uses a negative approach to presenting the story's deeper meaning. The underlying idea appears to be that the presentation of negative examples can be an important teaching device provided that it leads to beneficial results. The proviso is, of course, that the admonitions and warnings associated with such an undertaking are heeded. One such negative example is provided by the life cycle of the agave, a rare exotic flower. Its rapid growth and bloom, resulting in a floral display of breathtaking beauty, is accompanied by an equally speedy wilting and disintegration. Such—by way of a parallelism in human affairs—is the path of the phenomenal growth and rapid decline of the story's central character, an artist.

Marie Ebner's faith in the power and beneficial aspects of education and her consistent use of positive and negative examples are both a central feature and a propelling force in all of her stories. Yet faith alone does not suffice. Nor should one count solely on help from outside sources. In order to teach others well, one has to work on improving one's own level of knowledge and insight. To be sure, the author excelled in these areas of self-improvement. Like Gottfried Keller, she believed in being self-taught. But the entire process was unthinkable without the necessary discipline. To this point she writes in her late autobiographical volume *Aus einem zeitlosen Tagebuch* (From a Timeless Diary):

I spent all my life not only telling other people but

also telling myself: This is the way we are! Let us be
more rational and better. My preaching did the other
people no good. They just asked: What have we done
to her that she hates us so? They never noticed that I
preached to them out of love. I thus was of no use to
them. However, I was of use to myself. A bad preach-
er is the one who does not take *himself* to task. Well,
that much I can say because it is true: I have taken
myself to task.[34]

This excerpt makes clear as well that Marie Ebner believed
both reason and love to be integral as well as guiding forces
in her life and work.

Even in the last decade of her long life, she continued her
intellectual pursuits and her writing activities. Moreover, she
concentrated not only on books of remembrances and recollections but also on creative writing. In the former category,
though, she had published *Meine Kinderjahre,* the first of her
autobiographical volumes, already in 1906. In the following
year she went to Italy again for a while, staying primarily in
Venice. Two years later, in 1909, she finished and published
another book of aphorisms, to which she gave the title of
Altweibersommer (Indian Summer [literally: Old Women's
Summer]). The highly intellectual and parabolic sketches
contain a number of self-critical entries, in which she employs the power of irony. This text, in which she also did not
hesitate to poke fun at herself, was followed by her last two
collections of novellas, *Genrebilder* (Genre Pictures, 1910)
and *Stille Welt* (Quiet World, 1915). The latter book appears
on the surface to reflect on her own life, and it became her
literary swan song. However, the seemingly sedate and in-
ward looking title of the book is grossly misleading. Although close to death while putting the finishing touches on
it, Marie Ebner did not withdraw with unaccustomed sudden-

ness into a solipsistic world of her own. In fact, the outbreak of the First World War in August 1914, whose catastrophic ending for Austria she did not live to witness, caused her pain and dismay and cast a pall over the last two years of her life. Having resolved practically all of her life that love of others and service to her fellow human beings, irrespective of origin, was to be one of her highest personal goals, she looked with dismay and even disgust at the flood of nationalistic war poems, preaching hatred of other people. The second year of the war, moreover, became increasingly destructive and bloody. On the eastern front the loss of human lives in the battles at the Masurian lakes in the north and in Austrian Galicia in the south was exceedingly high on all sides. At the southern flank of its empire, Austria tried in vain to prevent Italy from joining the ranks of its opponents, the Grande Entente of France, England, and Russia, by showing its willingness to hand over the territory of the Trentino to the southern kingdom. Austria was still formally allied with Italy by a treaty agreement that included Germany and established—at least on paper—an alliance of the Central European powers. But Italy's resolve to join Austria's adversaries in battle could no longer be reversed. Italy, which Marie Ebner loved with an intensity reminiscent of that of Goethe, declared war on Austria-Hungary, accelerating thereby the foreseeable collapse and disintegration of the Danube monarchy. The immediate result of this political development was unsettling enough. The ensuing battles at the Isonzo proved increasingly costly in terms of human and material losses.

1916, the subsequent year of all-pervasive military conflict, brought a series of even more tragic events for Austria. Prime Minister Karl Graf Stürgkh was shot and killed by a son of Viktor Adler. The assassination was undertaken as a protest against the declaration of martial law by parliament. On the eastern front, Austria was struggling in intense battles against continuing massive attacks by huge Russian armies in the Carpathian mountains. The Russians almost succeeded in their attempt to overrun the area in order to threaten the Austrian heartland directly. The bloody confrontations at the Isonzo in the southern military theater continued. On November 21, 1916, the venerable Emperor Franz Joseph I died in the imperial residence of Schönbrunn. His death sealed not only the end of an epoch that had begun more than half a century before but—as it would soon become apparent—also the demise of the dream of the continuance of the multiethnic empire over which he presided. The installation of Archduke Karl—the Romulus Augustulus of the dying empire—as Emperor Karl I of Austria was incapable of reversing the disintegration process of the Danube monarchy, the inevitable result of the spreading forces of nationalism within its boundaries and an unwinnable war.

A few months before the death of the old emperor, Marie von Ebner-Eschenbach, herself mortally ill and deeply shaken by the unfolding debacle facing her country, had passed away on March 12, 1916. Her year of death, which she shared with Franz Joseph—as she had shared her year of birth and those of her marriage and loss of spouse—also witnessed the publication of two volumes of personal recollections, her booklet *Meine Erinnerungen an Grillparzer* (My Recollections of Grillparzer), in which she celebrated her decades-long association with her fatherly friend and benefactor, and the autobiographical work *Aus einem zeitlosen Tagebuch*. On December 11, a public commemoration was held in her honor at 7:30 p.m. at the *Festsaal des Ingenieur- und Architekten-Vereines* (Banquet Hall of the Society of Engineers and Architects) in the old city of Vienna. It was attended by her friends and many admirers. There, at the Eschenbachgasse 9, a moving commemorative address was given by Mathilde Countess zu Stubenberg. Maria Luggin, one of her most ardent and gifted devotées, read excerpts from her *Erinnerungen an Grillparzer, Aus einem zeitlosen Tagebuch, Das goldene Kleid* (The Golden Garment), *Aus meinen Kinderjahren, So ist es* (That is the Way It Is), and *Schattenleben* (Life in the Shadow).

This conspicuous public event added a measure of posthumous excitement to the seemingly uneventful life of Marie von Ebner-Eschenbach. But this outward appearance was vastly misleading. On closer scrutiny, it was not only her inner life that was full and intense. At a time when women's voices were conspicuously absent in the public and literary arenas of the German-speaking world, Marie Ebner's many books and stories are a proof of her resolve to contribute her part toward achieving a much-needed balance. As her fame and name recognition as a writer of national and international renown began to rise, she also became a nationally prominent voice and force in the Austrian democratic women's movement around the turn of the century. She felt very strongly that women deserved and needed to be heard on a personal as well as an intellectual level. Hers, however, was by no means a shrill voice of protest and accusation. She attempted to convey a message of love and understanding tempered in no small way by human reason. It is no exaggeration to suggest that the inner source of her creativity as a writer was her maternal instinct. Although life denied her children of her own, for which she inwardly longed, she was able as a writer to give of herself to many children and in return to receive from them their love and respect. The next chapter will give insight into the dramatic beginnings of her long and at times very tortuous struggle to establish herself as a woman writer in a man's world.

Chapter II

DRAMATIC BEGINNINGS

From time immemorial people have been enamored of public spectacles, whether grand displays, pageants, parades, or other such shows. In our own day, the human drive to see shows of some sort has, in fact, given birth to the multi-billion dollar video craze. The explanation of the popularity such spectacles elicit may be at least twofold. The urge of people to indulge their voyeuristic nature—which drive has in past ages been euphemistically described by religious and other philosophers as the *vita contemplativa,* a contemplation of life via inner or outer vision, in contrast to the so-called *vita activa*—betrays in part the desire to be entertained. A third element entering this equation of watching and enjoying life is that of vicariousness. Here, to be sure, the whole gamut of human emotions from the positive to the negative side of the emotive spectrum—love, compassion, sympathy, empathy, dislike, disgust, revulsion, fear, hatred—may become involved.

The nearly perfect vehicle of bringing these various human traits and urges together in one art form had proved to be the drama, one of the most ancient and popular forms of literary endeavor and expression. Both the religious and the secular origins of this art form and the word itself can be traced back to ancient Greece where the latter carried the connotation of "acting," "performing." While, viewed from the historical perspective, the drama as a literary genre in the

German-speaking lands lagged behind other Western European countries in its evolution—principally England and France, but also Spain—in the early 1840s, when Marie von Ebner-Eschenbach had her first contact with this art form while still a child, it had developed and matured fully, especially in Vienna, at the time not only the capital of the vast Austrian Empire, but also the foremost theater city in the entire German cultural sphere. The city and its expanding suburbs, in effect, had both: the numerous theaters and stages to satisfy an ever increasing public demand for this popular form of entertainment as well as a rapidly growing, rather sophisticated and highly critical theater-going public.

The drama and the theater go hand in hand. Although drama can be read, the genre lends itself readily and most naturally to theatrical performance. It is in the true sense of the word what it says it does and can consequently be fully appreciated only when performed on a stage in full view of an audience. Marie Ebner's first contacts with this literary genre were precisely along these lines. Only in later years did she take up reading dramas as a way of obtaining more extensive information about their structure and form. Her first visits to the Carl-Theater and the Theater an der Wien with her father, followed later by attendance of the Burgtheater, were to provide the incentive for her to begin experiments in this art form herself.

The Carl-Theater derived its name from the owner and director of the establishment, Karl Carl, who bought the theater in December 1838. It was already established and had the reputation of being the citadel of the *Altwiener Volkskomödie* (Old Viennese popular comedy). A suburban stage, officially called Theater in der Leopoldsstadt (Theater in Leopold City), it had in the previous century become popular as Kasperle-Theater. It obtained this name in the 1780s from its most popular performer in those days, the *Kasperl* (punch)

Johann Laroche. In his role as a Viennese version of the *Hanswurst* or stage buffoon, the principal comic figure of the play of the week—taken over from the Italian *commedia dell' arte*—provided the main entertainment of the performance and consequently became the theater's main drawing feature. In Marie Ebner's youth, this stage reached the high point of its artistic development after having undergone significant transformations in the first two decades of the nineteenth century under the auspices and directorships of Adolf Bäuerle, Josef Alois Gleich, and Karl Meisl, who were collectively called the "great threesome" of the Old Vienna popular theater. The two theatrical geniuses that brought the popular comedy performed on the stage of the Theater in der Leopoldsstadt to its highest flowering were Ferdinand Raimund, who has been called the "Viennese Shakespeare," and Johann Nepomuk Nestroy, his rival and successor, whom people dubbed the "Viennese Aristophanes." Both were not only theater impresarios, but also playwrights and stage performers in one, emulating thereby Shakespeare as well as Molière. Marie's father especially enjoyed Raimund's magical plays, the majority of which—Raimund wrote eight— were shown at the Theater in der Leopoldsstadt with the author directing and performing in the production.

Many of Raimund's plays, such as *Das Mädchen in der Feenwelt oder Der Bauer als Millionär* (The Girl in the World of the Fairies, or The Peasant as a Millionaire)—one of his most popular—were also shown at another Viennese stage of great renown, the Theater an der Wien. Marie Ebner refers to it and to Raimund's play in her autobiographical essay *Meine Kinderjahre* (My Childhood Years). This famous theater reached its artistic apex under the leadership of the theater genius Emanuel Schikaneder in the 1780s and 90s, when together with folksy farces, magic plays, and dramas of Lessing, Goethe, and Schiller even operas were performed on its stage. The most memorable performance was the first showing on September 30, 1791, of Mozart's comic opera *Die Zauberflöte* (The Magic Flute), to which Schikaneder also wrote the libretto. Another noteworthy performance on the stage of the Theater an der Wien was the first presentation of Beethoven's only opera *Fidelio*, on November 20, 1805.[1]

Marie's interest in the stage grew into an infatuation when her father began to take her regularly to the Burgtheater. Her love for this classical stage, soon developing into a passion, is a nearly perfect mirror-reflection of her own literary taste at the time, which went far beyond the folksy and popular into the higher artistic regions of cultural and intellectual entertainment. The origins of the Burgtheater go back to the early 1740s, when Empress Maria Theresa commissioned a theater entrepreneur by the name of Carl Selliers to convert the—at the time—empty imperial ball rooms on the Michaelerplatz (Square of Saint Michael) into a combined opera and theater that should also be open to the public. This combination stage could be reached from the imperial quarters by a direct passageway, hence its later name.[2] In 1776, Joseph II raised the status of this public theater "nächst der Burg" (next to the imperial castle) to "k.k. Hof- und Nationaltheater" (I.[mperial] [R.[oyal] Court [Theater] and National Theater). Under the leadership of the fabled Josef Schreyvogel,[3] Grillparzer's dramas were first performed on this stage. Heinrich Laube's later stewardship, so important to Marie Ebner in future years, brought the Burgtheater some much-needed stability and the reputation of remaining one of the premier repertory stages in the German-speaking world. Moreover, he helped to put into place its principal artistic goal, which was, simply stated, to become a repository of past dramatic traditions while at the same time being receptive to promising new theatrical trends.

Inspired by these theater visits, which began at the age of nine and intensified after she was twelve to the point that they became standard features during her stays in Vienna, Marie Ebner—still Marie Dubsky at the time—began to compose little plays in French and started even to perform in them with her sister and the small circle of close friends they both had. The choice of language should not come as a surprise considering her upbringing and the fact that she read Corneille, Racine, and the French classics enthusiastically and was even capable of reciting from them. In her autobiographical recollections *Meine Kinderjahre* she reflects on her first dramatic experiments:

> I became inexhaustible in inventing theatrical plays, which I did not write down but told in detail to my sister and our girlfriends and playmates. Friederike had no objection to this kind of activity. She even played a part when the decision was made to put my comedy on. . . . One Sunday, we experienced the strangest surprise. Our best actress . . . came in with a triumphant expression on her rosy face and a manuscript in her tender hands and told us that she had composed a play and had written it down.
>
> God, was that possible? To write a whole play?— My Lord, this girl Fanny. Who would have thought her capable of such a thing! (Hafis, 12:257-258).

Whether because of being inspired by her friend or on account of inclinations of her own, Marie attempted to write a play about Cinq-Mars, the confidant of Louis XIII, and his great opponent Richelieu. Doubtless, her early and enthusiastic reading of history had also helped to lay the groundwork for her ambitious task. In *Meine Kinderjahre* she relates her basic plan in some detail:

> . . . the first volume of the *Recollections, Serving as the Biography of Anna of Austria, Spouse of Louis XIII, King of France* by Madame de Motteville provided me with a magnificent topic for a drama which I developed ever more elaborately in the course of time. . . . Cinq-Mars was my hero; the young, reckless, naive favorite of Louis XIII, who wants to free his overlord from the crushing tyranny of the all-powerful minister Richelieu, succumbs in the boldly undertaken struggle with the giant, and dies magnificently after a moment of despair. (Hafis, 12:346)

But her plan did not stop here. It goes into additional deliberations about the play's main characters and the unfolding and denouement of its plot:

> And the magnificent characters that are shown along with [Cinq-Mars]: Louis XIII . . . a royal figure, imbued with narrow-mindedness; disloyal like weakness itself, harsh like intolerance. And ultimately he offers his two small sons to the triumphant cardinal as assurance of his total subjugation. But at this point, the queen rises in defiance and saves "the children of France" from the shame threatening them. I loved Queen Anna of Austria. . . . She ought to be portrayed as a heroine, who had boldly and proudly rejected the lion in love with her, simply because he dared to woo her as a woman. . . . But Richelieu should by all means become the highlight of the action. . . . The man who put his France ahead of all other countries on earth. . . . strove for literary fame. (Hafis, 12:347-348)

Still, Marie's ambitious plan to write her own play failed. The task proved to be beyond her youthful talent. By her own admission she struggled with the material for years, hoping for a breakthrough but not achieving one. The number of partial and unfinished manuscripts continued to grow, reflecting the changing focus of thematic approach and story line. While giving her first attempts at writing a historical drama the title "Cinq-Mars," she titled her last efforts in this unfinished enterprise "Richelieu." Finally, as she stated in later years, she burned the results of her protracted, yet fruitless struggle with the entire topic. To his surprise, Anton Bettelheim, Marie von Ebner-Eschenbach's first important biographer, discovered a discarded manuscript entitled "Richelieus Ende: Trauerspiel in fünf Akten" (Richelieu's End: Tragedy in Five Acts) in the Ebner-Eschenbach archives in Zdislawitz. It contained several acts of the play in a variety of versions. This account seems to provide proof that some sheets of her numerous drafts had escaped destruction after all.

Be that as it may, the glowing embers of her youthful ambition to become a playwright were not to be extinguished in her psyche for the next two decades. Although there appears to be no consistent record of the number and intensity of the dramatic sketches Marie Ebner may have undertaken in the first quiet years of her marriage from 1850 to 1858 in Klosterbruck, she was encouraged enough to write a full-fledged tragedy about the Scottish queen Mary Stuart in 1860. Calling it *Maria Stuart in Schottland,* she completed it in the short interval of three weeks, had it published, and sent it to a number of German theaters with the intent and the hope of having it performed on the stage. Both her studies of Robertson's history of Scotland and Schiller's drama *Maria Stuart,* to which her play provides an intended chronological preamble, had inspired her to write the historical drama. To her surprise and delight, the play was accepted by the Hofbühne

(Court Theater) of Karlsruhe. Eduard Devrient, its famous director—a student of Ludwig Tieck and a well-known historian of the German stage—intended to put it on there. Although not performed elsewhere for any length of time, it became a part of the Karlsruhe theater repertory.

In the drama's principal character, Marie Ebner had found a perennial stage favorite. Mary Stuart was one of the most tragic figures in the annals of Western history. This beautiful and artistically gifted woman was born on December 8, 1542, as the daughter of King James V of Scotland and his second wife, Mary of Lorraine, daughter of Claude, Duke of Guise, and widow of Louis of Orleans, Duke of Longueville. Both her Catholicism and her partial French origin generated enough resentment and prejudice in her Protestant homeland to be largely responsible for the tragic life of this brilliant but mostly unhappy woman. They were, in effect, the main reason why this great-granddaughter of Henry VII and granddaughter of Henry VIII, by law of succession eligible to assume not only the queenship of Scotland, but also that of England, became almost from birth a victim of a series of intrigues which ultimately were to lead to her premature and cruel death by beheading. Other contributing factors leading to her downfall were that she was by contrast to her cousin and rival for power, Queen Elizabeth of England, too emotional, given to hasty decisions, and incapable of securing the assistance and permanent support of the most powerful men in both Scotland and England to achieve ultimate success. Married off at the age of sixteen to the youthful but feeble Dauphin of France—who was to ascend the French throne as Francis II one year later, yet died ahead of the event—she was soon pushed out of France by the political wiles of the queen mother, Catharine de' Medici, who grasped the reins of power for her other son, Charles IX. On Mary's return to Scotland to assume her rightful reign as queen there, she was immediately victimized by the intrigues of a number of ambitious and ruthless men who were driven by the common goal of wanting to rule with or without her consent. Chief among them, next to her half-brother James Stuart, whom she elevated to be earl of Murray, was her cousin Henry Stuart, lord of Darnley and son of the earl of Lennox, whom she married in great haste against the advice of some of her most devoted followers. Her husband's worthlessness, arrogance, ambition, and folly were nearly matched by his baseness and debauchery. Yet he was to father her only son, who in later years was to become King James VI.

One year after the prince's birth in 1566, Darnley fell victim to a conspiracy against him. The house in which he slept was blown up and his lifeless body was found nearby. James Hepburn, earl of Bothwell, a reckless, vainglorious, and unprincipled adventurer, who enjoyed the queen's favor after she broke off relations with her husband, appeared to be the chief conspirator. When the queen married this man, whom everybody regarded as her husband's murderer, only three months after the deed was done, the Protestant nobles rose in rebellion against the couple in 1568, and Mary was forced to abdicate in favor of her infant son. Afterward, she felt compelled to flee to England and to ask Queen Elizabeth for protection, only to find herself a prisoner for life. But it took nearly twenty years for Elizabeth to find the courage to sign the warrant for the execution of her rival.

When Mary Stuart laid her head upon the block on February 8, 1587, with the dignity of a queen and the righteous resignation of a martyr, a historic legend was born. Here life and death were indeed the kind of stuff which lent itself naturally to the writing of grand tragedy. European drama seized upon it almost immediately after her death. As early as 1593, a Jesuit play entitled *Stuarta Tragoedia* by a certain Adrian de Roulers was written. This drama, together with many other such plays that followed it, has strong religious and didactic connotations. The main focus of all these early tragedies is on the martyrdom of the Catholic queen. The French playwright Antoine de Montchrestien was the first to portray Mary Stuart as a beautiful and enticing enchantress in his lyrical and elegiac play *L'Ecossoise ou Le desastre,* written in 1605. The much better known Spanish dramatist Félix Lope de Vega Carpio, on the other hand, relates the story of Mary Stuart bereft of all poetic embellishment in his *Corona trágica, vida y muerte de la Serenissima Regina de Escocia, Maria Estuarda* of 1627. He presents the queen as a Catholic saint and depicts her opponent Elizabeth as a creature of the devil. The English playwright John Banks, however, was the first to drop the heretofore popular antithetical portrayal of both queens, as dictated by their different and opposing religious creeds, in favor of a more even-handed approach. His *The Island Queen or Mary Queen of Scots* of 1648 is, in fact, an attempt to explain their mutual antagonism along psychological lines.

A new story line was introduced by M. Regnault in his *Marie Stuart, rein d'Ecosse,* written in 1639. He places a man between the two queens, who then becomes the cause of their rivalry. Two seventeenth-century German versions, which also had some influence on Schiller's *Maria Stuart,* are J. Reimer's *Von hohen Vermählungen* (Of Noble Marriages) of 1579 and A. von Haugewitz's *Schuldige Unschuld oder Maria Stuarda* (Guilty Innocence or Mary Stuart) of 1683. Schiller's drama, considered by many to be the most artistically satisfying version of the life and death of the ambivalent Scottish queen, summarizes plot variants of the preceding two hundred years and integrates them into a unified, well balanced whole. At the climax of the tragedy, first performed at the Weimar Court Theater in 1800, Maria not only triumphs over Elisabeth but also—by conquering her baser self, accepting her imminent death without rancor, and even forgiving her adversary—transforms herself into a "beautiful soul" in the Schillerian sense. Marie Ebner's own portrayal of the tragic queen was doubtless most profoundly influenced by Schiller's depiction of her character. Later well known versions of the Mary Stuart story, such as the Norwegian variant of Bjørnstjerne Bjørnson's *Maria Stuart i Skotland* and Swinburne's elaborate trilogy, *Chastelard, Bothwell,* and *Mary Stuart,* postdate Marie Ebner's own treatment of this popular topic.[4]

No matter how one judges the literary and dramatic value of *Maria Stuart in Schottland,* which was first published as a book in 1860, two facts remain indisputable. The drama represents a first and, considering its popular topic, courageous foray into the realm of a long and continuing tradition by a woman. Moreover, by writing it and presenting it to the public, Marie Ebner enters simultaneously the august sanctum of a literary genre, which at the time was still thought to be the apogee of literary endeavor and was nearly universally practiced and controlled by men. Stated more simply, her brave entry as a woman writer into the dramatic field places her in a long line of male competitors, who have dealt with the tragedy of a woman of royal lineage caught and eventually destroyed in the web of male intrigue and lust for power. Her version consequently deserves special attention, inasmuch as it uniquely records a woman's point of view.

Marie Ebner opens the expository part of her five-act play in Holyrood. There the queen, already married to Darnley, has been incarcerated. What is worse, her residence is occupied by the assassins of Rizio, her former chancellor and confidant. Both the king, who feared a rival in Rizio for the queen's favors, and the earl of Murray were conspirators in the murder plot. Darnley proposes now to share power with Murray provided that the latter supports the queen's removal

from power. Murray, the queen's "natural" brother, decries
Darnley's cowardice, treachery, and weakness:

> Oh hypocrite! Just put your fear into the
> Attire of a grandmother—. . .
> You shadow of a king—a woman's
> Creature!—Hence carry your ignominious burden,
> If you do not have the strength to rid yourself of it!
> You have been born and conceived to be a servant;
> No royal blood flows in your veins![5]

But Murray pursues political plans of his own. It becomes
evident that Maria Stuart is surrounded by ambitious and un-
trustworthy men vying to enhance their own status and
power. There appears to be only one exception to the lot of
them, one honest man: the aged earl of Lennox, Darnley's
father. Nonetheless, Maria Stuart still puts her trust in her
husband. She hopes that Darnley will help to crush the conspiracy against her, not least for their son's sake. But the
king will have none of it and accuses her of having been unfaithful to him. She denies her alleged guilt. Her last will and
final testament will reveal her innocence. In case of her death
Darnley will become regent of Scotland until their son comes
of age. The Scottish lords approach the queen now and promise her freedom if she will agree to safeguard the reformed
church, discontinue her Catholic services in the realm, share
power with the king, and pardon the earl of Murray and all
those who have taken part in Rizio's assassination. Marie refuses her consent but asks the lords to reveal the name of
their leader. At this crucial juncture, Bothwell enters and
frees the queen. Even though it seems beyond doubt now that
her own husband headed the conspiracy against her, Darnley
denies it over the objections of the other rebellious lords. The
queen chooses to believe him, yet orders the other conspira-

tors to be incarcerated. She also welcomes her brother back.

In act two, Darnley becomes fully aware of Murray's duplicity and cruelty. The latter mocks Darnley's lack of resolve openly now. The queen, in the meantime, wishes to confer with counts Bedfort and Brieune, ambassadors of England and France. On meeting with them she is comforted by France's continuing support of her claim to the English throne, contested and denied her by England's present queen, Elisabeth. Bedfort on leaving whispers to Murray: "She sharpens the arrow / Which will pierce her through and through" (20). Murray's reply: "Let her sharpen it . . . / I will tighten the bow, which will send it!" (20) reveals his stand in this dispute. Outwardly, however, he feigns fidelity to the queen. Darnley meanwhile, realizing that his fortunes are slipping, pleads for leniency for all the conspirators. The queen relents in her resolve to punish them severely and pardons the Scottish lords Douglas, Ruthven, and Kerr. Privately, however, she now accuses Darnley of treachery. Convinced of his dishonesty and guilt, she reveals her innermost feelings:

> I can not listen to your voice any longer.
> I hate and despise your countenance.
> I hate you! I hate myself—for
> Having ever loved you! (21)

Bothwell appears to be the main power behind Maria Stuart's throne now. She has, in fact, put all her trust in him:

> Yes, you are true and warm and will never
> Betray me, though I have given you nothing,
> Though I am to you—only: the queen! (21)

At this point, Bothwell openly declares his love for her as a man. Deeply smitten herself, she elevates him to be "Margrave of Scotland" (26).

The third act, traditionally the climax of German Classical drama, reveals that Maria has deeply fallen in love with Bothwell. Darnley sees himself surrounded by enemies. While he fears death, his erstwhile antagonist Murray appears well entrenched. He warns Maria that Elisabeth, allegedly afraid of Maria's popularity among her own Catholic subjects, plans to attack Scotland in order to oust her. Despite the apparent imminent danger, Maria professes her peaceful intentions. She wants to reconcile her differences with the English queen. Though privately expressing his disdain for Bothwell, his latest rival for power, Murray accuses Darnley of high treason before the queen. Behind her back, however, he plans to kidnap the infant crown prince. It is Darnley's and Bothwell's turn now to engage in a heated argument, in the course of which the king expresses his hatred for both his rival for the queen's favors and for the queen herself. Bothwell is incensed, and implores Maria to command him to kill Darnley. But the queen counsels caution and forgiveness. He is, after all, the father of her child. She forces Bothwell to give her his word to spare Darnley. However, Bothwell has no intention of keeping it. When one of his supporters, Lord Ruthven, offers his services to kill Darnley, Bothwell readily agrees. Murray, in the meantime, continues to pursue his own aims. He urges Maria to dismiss Bothwell. He wants to be the queen's right hand himself. Not surprisingly, she rejects his offer. Feeling uncertain and betrayed, she seeks succor in God. Soon word reaches her that the king's residence has been blown up. He is most likely dead. Maria rejects Lennox's accusation that Bothwell is the murderer.

At the beginning of act four, Maria's faithful lady in waiting, Lady Argyll, observes the queen in prayer. Reflecting on her mistress, she considers her innocent of all wrongdoing but badly threatened nonetheless. Bothwell will have to face trial before the court of lords and prove his innocence in the king's death. Lady Argyll professes her devotion for and fidelity to the queen. The latter reflects on Bothwell:

> Compared to him, the princely prodigal,
> I remain for all times and eternity
> A poor, niggardly, powerless woman. (41)

Four months after Darnley's death, the high court convenes to pass judgment. Lennox accuses Bothwell of being his son's murderer. Yet he lacks the proof to convict him. The lord judges consequently declare Bothwell innocent. Frustrated to the point of being enraged, Lennox attacks Bothwell physically before the assembled. Maria attempts to intervene but is accused by Lennox in turn of being part of the conspiracy that victimized his son. In the ensuing struggle Bothwell overwhelms Lennox. Generous as always, Maria saves his life by ordering him to leave the country. The lords now order her to also banish Bothwell and to send him into exile as well. Instead, she thoughtlessly provokes the lords' anger by elevating Bothwell to be her husband. After this pivotal turning point, Murray sarcastically pays homage to the queen's new consort by entoning his new title: "Hail Duke Orkney!" (49).

In the fifth and final act of the drama the lords gather to form an opposition against Bothwell. The earl of Mar is the organizer of the opposing forces. Their avowed aim is not only to dispose of Bothwell and the queen, but also to protect the rights of the crown prince. Maria, although shaken, is now willing to fight for her throne:

> They ask themselves? They dare. Oh! Tell them:
> Where their queen is, there is justice!

> Issue a proclamation to my people:
> — Every one, who calls himself faithful and
>   honorable (pointing to Bothwell):
> Let him follow this man! If he calls to do battle.
>   . . . (52)

But Murray brings bad tidings. The people side with the opposing lords. Still, Maria had no regrets:

> . . . If God were to put in my right hand
> All the royal crowns on earth,
> — In my left hand, Bothwell's hand and were to
>   say: "Choose:—
> I would let go of all the crowns on earth
> And would go with him . . . (53)

Bothwell tries in vain to stop the opposing forces. His army flees. All is lost. He now tells Maria that her brother Murray has joined the camp of their enemies. The few remaining faithful fighters want to be led by lord Huntly. Lord Iverness implores Bothwell, now Duke of Orkney, to save Maria, but Bothwell rejects this suggestion. He seems to be preoccupied with his own safety. When Maria wants Bothwell to be by her side, she learns at last of his duplicity. At this point of no return, he also admits to her his complicity in Darnley's death and flees like a coward. Maria is taken prisoner again. She has no other recourse but to give up her crown in favor of her son. In despair she resolves to flee to England, to Elisabeth. Murray offers his assistance. Huntly's words of warning: "To Your worst enemy?!" (63) are of no avail. She is ready to depart now. Murray cruelly refuses her final request for permission to see her son. Her parting words convey the depth of her feelings:

To—Elisabeth!
— Then fare well, you place of sorrows,
Oh Scottish soil, once subordinate to me!
. . . .
Oh native soil, my tears kiss,
And my lips, your holy ground.
And: Blessings! Blessings are my final prayer,
And fervent repentance every breath!— (64)

Murray triumphs at the end. He is now regent of Scotland.
His plot has succeeded. Maria is on her way to England.
Lord Bedfort's final words anticipate Schiller's play:

She seeks shelter there and finds a judge!
It is for her the path to the scaffold of blood.— (64)

Thus ends this remarkable play of reason and love gone
astray. Ignored today, it nevertheless confirms rather than
contradicts Eduard Devrient's high opinion of Marie Ebner's
talent as a dramatist. In her development of the drama's plot
she made good use of her historical sources. She barely deviated from the historical tradition in this, her first completed
dramatic effort. This implies by no means, however, that she
was unbiased in her thematic treatment of the plot. But her
subjectivity in presenting Maria Stuart in a favorable light
goes beyond Schiller's sympathy in at least two ways. Ebner-
Eschenbach's Maria Stuart appears to be a victim of her own
tendency to put faith in others. Because of her trusting disposition, she is consistently betrayed and victimized by men of
ambition and violence. First Darnley and later Bothwell take
advantage of her naive belief that their actions were guided
by genuine love for her. But—as the last lines of the drama
indicate—in spite of her negative experiences and bitter disappointments, Maria is still not prepared to forsake her faith

in the inherent kindness and even goodness of the human species. In her relations with others she continues to be guided by her own inner sense of ethical feeling. Almost blindly, she entrusts her future fate and well-being to Elisabeth, in whose kingdom and at whose court she expects to find a safe haven.

This naive optimism, however, is not to be misconstrued as being simply and solely an indicator of the immature naivete on the part of the heroine or even the authoress herself, projecting her own inner feelings into her protagonist. Doubtless one of the reasons why Marie Ebner chose this historic figure in the first place had to do with her intent to link the emblematic quality of her heroine's fate with the contemporary treatment of women as well as the inequality in the relations between males and females. The authoress, in effect, may have been tempted to depict the fate of all women in that of the unfortunate Scottish queen. Thus she raised her voice not only on behalf of one historic figure of tragic proportions—whom she portrayed as basically blameless, albeit naive and passionate—but, in a symbolic sense, with all women in mind, at the behest, so to speak, of the entire sex. At any rate, this way of looking at Marie Ebner's first play would also blunt Otto Ludwig's largely negative remarks about the play, who for years had himself harbored the plan of writing a drama about "King Darnley." Ludwig criticized "Mister Eschenbach's" efforts to present an apotheosis of the heroine as a biographical rather than as a dramatic feature. Yet even Ludwig felt obliged to praise the "author's" stylistic acumen and rhetorical force. The skill, in fact, which Marie Ebner employs in her use of blank verse in this drama goes demonstrably beyond the epigonic.[6]

If there was any doubt about Marie Ebner's longing to identify herself, not only in sentiment, but also in name, with a heroine of her dramatic imagination, her second grand attempt at writing drama makes this need absolutely clear. She called this play *Marie Roland,* even though the historic figure after whom she named the tragedy went by the legal name of Manon Philipon Roland de la Platière, being the wife of the French entrepreneurial and political figure, Jean-Marie Roland de la Platière. Mary Stuart's tragic life touched Marie Ebner personally. She deeply sympathized and fully identified with her suffering, principally brought about by a cruel world incapable of creating safeguards to uphold a woman's rights and her personal integrity even if she was of royalty. By comparison Madame Roland's historical plight as a woman went one step further. It expanded into the area of modern political life and that of outright revolution. Her tragic life offered Marie Ebner more than personal and generic dimensions. It no longer reflected just on one person's struggle for her own happiness, fulfillment, and possible aggrandizement. Nor did it address itself solely to a woman's struggle to achieve equal rights for the members of her sex alone. As important and satisfying as these goals were, they no longer sufficed. Marie Ebner wanted to show a woman who was a wife, a mother, and a political leader in one. Her tragic death was to be the direct result of her willingness to sacrifice her life for the perceived betterment of all of humanity. The symbolism of this historic figure thus transcends her sex. In Marie Roland, the dramatist places before us a heroine of the French Revolution.

The historic Madame Roland was born in Paris on March 17, 1754. Her father Pierre Gratien Philipon was an engraver. She was a child of remarkable intelligence. Already at the age of four she developed a passion for reading. At seven she memorized a treatise on heraldry and was able to recite it at will. When she was eight she carried an edition of Plutarch to regular church service, read Tasso's *Jerusalem Delivered,* and fired her childish imagination digesting *Télémaque* of

Feuelon. All these intellectual activities did not in the least interfere with her ardent religiosity, which led her to enroll at the Maison des Dames de la Congrégation in the Faubourg Saint Marcel. Here she formed a close friendship with two schoolmates from Amiens, Henrietta and Sophie Cannet, which, especially in the case of the latter, proved to be very fruitful in later years. After two years of schooling at the Maison, she returned home and experienced a remarkable intellectual change. She lost interest in religious writers, and the so-called defenders of the Bible and the church. The fervent religious faith of her earlier years gave way to the enlightened views of the *encyclopédistes* and *philosophes,* whose writings she began to devour. In her ethics she embraced the philosophy of stoicism. Shortly after her mother's death, she read Rousseau's *La Nouvelle Héloise,* which was to her—as it was to many of her generation—a true revelation. Because of tensions at home caused by the imprudent conduct of her father, she saw no other recourse but to withdraw to the Maison des Dames de la Congrégation again at the age of twenty-five. But Monsieur Roland, who had fallen in love with her and courted her for five years, rescued her from the austere life there by asking her for her hand in marriage. Although Roland, an inspector of manufactures at Amiens, was her elder by twenty years, the marriage, solemnized on February 4, 1780, proved to be happy and longlasting. Her husband, born at Mizy near Villefranche on February 18, 1734, and raised in this provincial setting, held the post of an inspector-ordinary at Amiens. He had met Manon Philipon at the house of Sophie Cannet, a mutual friend. By all accounts, it was love at first sight. He was smitten not only by her fascinating beauty, but also by her intellectual genius.

When the revolution of 1789 broke out, the couple became fervent partisans of the movement. In 1791 Monsieur

Roland was sent to Paris by the municipality of Lyons for the express purpose of representing the Lyon weavers, whose working conditions were deplorable, in the constituent assembly. When the assembly was dissolved the very same year, he founded the Club Central in Lyons. The members of this organization, soon calling themselves Rolandins, were known for their fervor for constitutional liberty. Toward the close of 1791, the couple returned to Paris, where Jean-Marie became one of the leaders of the Girondist or moderate wing of the republicans. In March 1791 he was appointed minister of the interior. He held that post until January 1793, when he resigned in despair after seeing that his moderate counsels were ignored. Briefly incarcerated after the radicalization of the assembly and the fall of his party, he was able to flee to Rouen.

But Manon, who was also arrested and imprisoned in the Abbaye, was forced to stay behind. Her dauntless and intrepid spirit there became legend. Released on the 24th of June, she was rearrested by the same commisar who had set her free before. Now she was confined in Saint Pelagie, where she spent her imprisonment in study and in the composition of her political *Mémoires*. Although no tangible accusations against her were ever raised, Madame Roland was summoned before the revolutionary tribunal in the beginning of November and was condemned to death. She was guillotined on November 9, 1793. It is said that she asked for a pen and paper while standing at the scaffold to write down "the strange thoughts that were passing through her head." Still more celebrated are words she spoke to the statue of liberty, at the foot of which the scaffold was erected: "O Liberty, what crimes are committed in thy name!" In another version, her final words are said to have been "Liberty, how they have played with the name!"[7] When news reached her husband of the execution of his wife, Monsieur Roland became so distraught that he committed suicide in the small village in the environs of Rouen, in which he was hiding, on November 14, 1793. The depth of his devotion to his wife is preserved in several memoirs and in six volumes of personal letters which he addressed to Manon before their marriage from Switzerland, Italy, Sicily, and Malta.[8]

Ebner-Eschenbach's *Marie Roland,* printed in 1867 and briefly performed in Weimar, is a five-act tragedy that focuses loosely on the most tragic period in Madame Roland's life: the last few weeks before her incarceration and death. In contrast to Georg Büchner's earlier drama *Dantons Tod* (Danton's Death), principally dealing with the disintegration of the French Revolution and the demise of one of its main initiators—a work which Marie Ebner may not have known—*Marie Roland* portrays in a positive way the high moral stature and inner strength of another of the Revolution's most outstanding personages.[9] Written in the irregular iambic verse of its predecessor drama, *Maria Stuart in Schottland,* with mostly five stresses to the line, but occasionally also showing interspersed trochaic verse, the play's action opens in the Roland apartment on the Rue la Harpe. Vergniaud, Gensonné. and Barbaroux, members of the Girondist or moderate republican wing in the French legislative assembly, reveal that Marie Roland is writing a plea for her husband who has been dismissed as a minister of the state. He was, as everybody agrees, an excellent scientist and an honest servant of the state and the people. Roland, on entering, protests his innocence. He has not misappropriated public funds. He states emphatically, moreover, that he will rebuff Hébert's challenge and accusations in the Convention. Rather than forsake his faith in the republic, he is prepared to die:

I want to die like Cato and like Brutus,

> On the day which robs me of all my faith
> In your future—free republic![10]

Marie, who has joined in the discussion, disagrees:

> Who speaks of dying before his work is done?
> Was your aim only to destroy injustice
> When you overturned the structure of the
>   monarchy?
> There was a higher aim! The aim was to establish
>   justice,
> A new law in a newly funded empire.
> The great work is still unfinished.
> It summons you—well, here you stand! (5)

Vergniaud calling Marie the very soul of the opposition—
"You are the soul of the Gironde and always / Your wish
seemed to be law"(5)—proposes that an alliance be sought
with Danton. Marie rejects this proposition in a spirit of both
courage and defiance. She calls on the faithful to fight, to occupy the Convention, and to arrest Danton and Robespierre
as well:

> Go there—gain that in battle
> For which the people feverishly and vainly struggle:
> Peace in freedom! (8)

Privately she confesses that, although a married woman, she
fell in love with Buzot. When the latter, also a member of
the Girondists, enters she pleads with him to flee the house,
which is surrounded. They profess their love for each other,
but Marie admonishes restraint. Armed Sansculottes enter
now, search the house and threaten Marie, only to leave without harming her.

In act two Marie's friend and confidante Lodoïska brings
Marie a letter, which reveals that Hébert has been arrested.
It also states that Buzot is confronting their common enemies, the Jacobins, in the Convention and facing them brave-
ly. Lodoïska, on her part, has breached the laws of society by
leaving her husband for a lover. Marie shows understanding:
"Much is forgiven the one who is much loved" (12). Yet
after her friend departs, she argues with her inner self regarding her own feelings of love and sees no other recourse but
to condemn herself:

> . . . I hate you,
> Forbidden luck—you poisonous reptile,
> That only devours the heart—I hate you! (12)

Her daughter Eudora relates, on entering, the harrowing story
of her escape from a marauding mob. A royalist, the old
count Beugnot, saved her from disgrace and has accompanied
her home. He calls Marie: "The queen of the Gironde" (13).
Marie, left alone, doubts her calling to leadership. She longs
for happiness with Buzot. In the city, hell has broken loose.
Hébert's incarceration caused the mob to rise in rebellion.
They storm the Convention. Marie beseeches Buzot not to
sacrifice his life. The latter wants Roland to flee with wife
and child. Roland declines. He insists on facing his accusers
in order to seek satisfaction. Marie confesses to Roland her
love for Buzot. Her infatuation is an open secret, however.
People had noticed it and were talking about it in derogatory
terms. Nonetheless, the older man not only forgives her, but
also offers his wife her freedom. Yet she rejects his generous
offer. She wants to stand by his side in his hour of need and
be faithful to him as well.

Act three takes place in the Convention. Lacroix and Le-
gendre, two adherents of the Jacobin faction, note that the

Girondists defend their reactionary views stubbornly. Marat joins in calls for extreme measures against the Girondists, who appear doomed at this point. Danton counsels them to resign their mandates. After they refuse, he asks rhetorically:

> Why don't you choose a man as your leader?
> . . . .
> That woman will destroy you—she is the
> Circe of the Revolution. (18)

Robespierre has warned them before. In private, however, the three radical leaders of the Revolution berate one another. Marat and Robespierre have their different, though violent, objectives. Danton, talking to Lacroix about them, calls Robespierre "the ghost" and Marat "the tiger." Counting on his own popularity, he intends to survive them both. In a later scene Danton confronts Marie, who has come to enter the Convention despite previous objections on the part of Lacroix. She is without fear, however, and rejects Danton's offer to make peace and to forge a political alliance together. His plea is in vain:

> I bring what you are lacking: strength . . .
> Thousand heads may meet in counsel.
> Only one hand can act. You need the hand
> Which puts a bridle on the rough mob,
> That gives direction to the Convention
> And the nation the impetus to victory.
> By all means grasp it! (22)

Marie rejects his offer in disgust:

> You don't believe in the people and kneel down
> before them?

—Well, look! We succumb to them and still love
  them!
We fall—our faith stands firm! (23)

At the end of the act, Robespierre also expresses his disgust
with Danton. But he does it for a different reason. Danton
has become too powerful. The people are enamored of him:
"The republic needs neither a lord nor an idol" (24).

In the fourth act the action returns to the apartment of the
Rolands. Buzot relates that the Committee of Twelve has
been disbanded, and the Girondists have been indicted for
high treason. It is obvious that the whole Convention has
given in to the wishes of the bloodthirsty mob and vies to
curry favor with it. Barbaroux calls on his fellow Girondists
to fight. Roland speaks out against meeting force with force.
It would mean civil war. But Marie throws all caution to the
wind: "Are we made of stone?—There is no standing still!"
(27). Moreover, she is not afraid of the tyrants:

. . . the people love me.
[The radicals] wouldn't dare touch me;
But if they were in senseless delusion,
I would not climb onto the scaffold a harmless
  victim.
My gushing blood would incite revenge
In many thousand hearts, which hesitate fearfully
  now.
. . . Oh Danton, Danton, I am tempted,
Mightily tempted to show you, you devil,
How heavy a head weighs on the scale of fate,
In which a divine thought has lived! (27)

After these powerful words are spoken, Roland professes his
sadness and shock. He is profoundly concerned about his

wife's future safety. He fears, in effect, for her life:

> With my wife they'd kill
> The best that was my own: love,
> And leave me only with hatred for France. . . .
> Because I don't ever want to learn to hate my
>   people,
> I have to die the very same day. . . . (28)

Marie, for her part, does not fear for her life. Her plight, as she sees it, lies in the fact that she is a woman and that she cannot act freely: "Bound, firmly and eternally chained / To duty! . . . Impotent woman!" (28) After her husband's departure, she questions God's mercy, which Buzot implored:

> —If I were a god and were compassionate,
> There would be no creature in my world
> Whose heart be as torn as is,
> Alas, this very one!—(29)

Her doubts about herself dissipate, however, when three members of the Insurrection Committee, accompanied by guards and a justice of the peace, place her under arrest. Upon the latter's remark: "You are much beloved," she replies firmly: "I am beloved. Yes—because I love in turn!" (30).

The locale of act five is Marie's prison cell. Her maid Sophie has been permitted to bring Marie flowers. The two reflect on the fate of Marie Antoinette. Lodoïska, who has also been allowed to visit Marie, reveals her plan to free her. She also relates the sad news of Roland's death by his own hand on hearing of Marie's alleged execution. Lodoïska offers to take Marie's place in prison to facilitate her escape. Marie is overwhelmed by her friend's devotion:

You, the better one of [the two of] us, before whom
   I humble myself!—
For the first time before a human being.
For the first time also in true humility
Before the god who spoke to me through you!—
Compassionate one, whom I've blasphemously
   disavowed
And who so magnificently manifests himself before
   me.
I am prostrating myself in the dust. I acknowledge
   you!
I am a poor, errant creature.
Most benevolent one! Father! Judge!—be gracious
   to me! (35)

Lacroix, representing the Committee, prepares Marie mentally
for her execution now. She asks Lodoïska to care for her
child. Convinced of the righteousness of her cause, she ap-
proaches death with courage:

The task is divine—human beings complete it.
. . . .
The thirst for justice is in the hearts of millions;
Humanity fights for it in this one nation! (36)

To Lacroix she exclaims at the end: "I am returning to God
/ Not to the church" (36).

It is clear from the very outset of the tragedy to its denouement that the author deviated greatly in the development
of her story line from the historic version of the lives and
roles of both Rolands, husband and wife, in the French Revolution. Not only did she overstate the historic role of her
heroine in comparison to that of the latter's husband, but she
also took great liberties, among others, in the depiction of her

heroine's amorous attachment in the center of the plot and in portraying her husband's suicide toward the end, which historically did not precede her execution but followed it. These observations, however, should by no means be misconstrued as criticism. Marie Ebner's deviations from the sources of her historical background confirm rather than contradict the fact that historic fiction is just that. Her tragedy about the heroic stance of a woman leading to her death and her apotheosis transcends, in fact, the historic background. It is Marie Ebner's most personal work. She rewrote part of it after the first printing and had the revision inserted in the text. In particular and notwithstanding the Schillerian overtones in her heroine's character development, the play places this much admired figure of the French Revolution before us not only in her generic role as a heroic woman who sacrifices her personal happiness and even her life for a larger good, but also as a thinly disguised autobiographical poetization of Marie Ebner's own earlier experiences in Klosterbruck.

Seen from this perspective, in effect, the play becomes a personalized drama à clef, in the psychological core of which the author, her husband Moritz, and their mutual friend Weilen form a proverbial love triangle. Roland, like Moritz, is much older than the heroine. Moreover, Marie Ebner depicts him in the mold of her own husband as a technical-minded person and a scientist rather than as the leader of a political movement. In both instances, in real life as in the play, the bond between husband and wife is that of friendship and mutual respect rather than that of fervent love. Marie's more passionate attachment, albeit platonic and nonsexual, is reserved for her idealistic friend. In the drama, Marie Roland, inflamed by this love, sacrifices her life for the mutually shared ideal of justice and peace in freedom. In real life, Marie Ebner's psychic love for Weilen leads in the Freudian sense to the breakthrough in her that ultimately enables her to become a writer. In both instances, however, the inner conflict is that between the Schillerian concept of duty and inclination. Marie Ebner, as a dramatist and as a woman, was obviously deeply beholden to and influenced by Schiller's *Weltanschauung* and ideology. In the sense that both she and her heroine overcome the deep-seated desire that tempted them to succumb to their inner needs for erotic fulfillment and strictly follow the dictates of duty to do what is proper and morally right, the play and real life coalesce. In Marie Roland, the author therefore did not just choose a historic personage that reflected her own sense of womanhood at its most idealistic. She also unveiled in this dramatic character a heretofore well-hidden part of her inner self. The French writer Lamartine, whom Ebner knew and respected, described this heroine of the French Revolution, whom Goethe had also admired, as a fervent disciple of truth. In the circle of her family as well as in the public limelight of the political arena, she fights the seamy, destructive, and self-immolating side of the revolution, from the ideals of which she had expected so much good to come. In spite of all disappointments she upholds her own ideals, however, to the very end and ascends the guillotine in a resigned and collected manner.

Thus Marie Ebner's heroine adheres to the principles of free will, overcoming guilt—again in the mold of Schillerian idealism—and giving her imminent death thereby a higher meaning. Ultimately she is the opposite of the passive female protagonists of the later German Naturalist movement, whose actions have been predetermined by heredity and environment, nor can she be compared with Hebbel's blameless tragic heroines, who are caught between the overpowering demands of an older social order and the as yet unattainable promise of a more benign future whose coming their tragic demise purportedly foreshadows. Marie Ebner's contemporaries Louise von François and Paul Heyse praised *Marie Roland* as a work of touching nobility and power. Friedrich Halm, who after Laube's dismissal was to become general manager of the Burgtheater, wrote Ebner enthusiastically in 1867: "Whosoever, after reading *Marie Roland*, should still doubt your talent, is an imbecile or an envious person."[11] But wary of the censors and the political consequences, neither he nor his predecessor Laube had dared to perform the play on stage. It was just too much of a risk, as Eduard Devrient had also realized in Karlsruhe. For *Marie Roland* is not only a highly personal play almost inadvertently revealing some of the hidden psychological secrets of Marie Ebner. It is above all a political play with a clearly discernible political and social message that was not well received by the authorities.

After this outward failure, temporary success was to set in again two years later in 1869, when Marie Ebner submitted a solicited contribution to the Wiener Schiller-Fonds (Schiller Foundation of Vienna), which she was able to complete in one week. She titled the dramatic poem resulting from this effort *Doktor Ritter*, the pseudonym Schiller used while hiding in Bauerbach after having fled his native Württemberg in 1782 and having found only temporary haven in Mannheim. The one-act play, comprised of six scenes, was so well received at its initial performance at the Festakademie (Festival Academy) in Vienna that the Burgtheater showed an interest in it and performed it five times. The action takes place in Bauerbach in 1783. Schiller is twenty-four. This is a most crucial and insecure time in his life. In 1778, the historic Schiller had completed the first sketch of his drama *Die Räuber* (The Robbers) while still studying medicine at the Karlsschule (Carl School) under the watchful eye of the duke of Württemberg, who had sponsored his studies there since 1773. On its publication in 1780 the play elicited a great deal of enthusiasm among the young all over Germany. They were enthralled with the passions displayed in it. The older generation, dignitaries and functionaries, on the other hand, were deeply disturbed and even scandalized. The duke himself, a very conservative man, forbade Schiller to write any more such "poetry" without submitting it to his inspection.

When *Die Räuber* saw its first performance on the stage in Mannheim in 1782, Schiller attended it secretly without obtaining official permission to do so from any of his superiors. As a result he was placed under arrest for a fortnight on his return to Stuttgart. This led to still further complications. Ultimately, he fled from the harsh supervision of the duke to Franconia in late September of the same year and lived the following year under an assumed name in Bauerbach, near Meiningen, as the guest of Henrietta von Wolzogen. His stay there proved to be very productive. He completed his *Verschwörung des Fiesco in Genua* (Conspiracy of Fiesco in Genoa), relating the Genoese dream of a republican democracy and its failure, and his bourgeois tragedy *Kabale und Liebe* (Intrigue and Love), a strong condemnation of the corrupt and conceited aristocratic ruling class and the unjust practices of the *ancien régime* over which it presided. He also sketched his *Don Carlos,* with which play, later changed and rewritten in a more mature style,[12] he completed his first poetic development, a phase known as his *Sturm und Drang* (storm and stress) period.[13]

Marie Ebner's short play, also written in the formal style of German Classical drama, provides less of a focus, however, on the literary and philosophical implications of this formative phase in Schiller's overall development than it does on the story of his unrequited love. The central and pivotal core of the play's plot, in fact, is the young author's unhappy love for Charlotte von Wolzogen, the young daughter of his benefactress. His main opponent is the influential manager of the estate, Vogt, who counsels the baroness against the liaison between her daughter and a mere poet, who in addition to being a commoner is also a political radical. She should marry an equal. Convinced of the correctness of this argument, the mother consequently rebuffs the poet when he expresses his love for Charlotte to her:

> The cheerful girl with the gentle soul:
> Her life must flow tenderly and quietly,
>
> . . . .
> But you have no peace to offer.
> Fighting is your way of life.
> In you the worldly genius strives to assert itself.
> Brought back to life, a new spirit of the age
> Wants to manifest itself through you.
> It comes in the throes of storms, in thunderous
>   clouds—,
> You are its priest, its prophet, you![14]

Her words are a terrible blow to Schiller's hope for his future by the side of the woman he loves. Torn between the moral urge to pursue his high calling as a poet and writer—a self-imposed inner directive—and the natural inclination of any young person to achieve personal happiness through love and unable to resolve this psychological dilemma, he is willing in a spate of depression to forsake his dramatic career altogether and to make peace with Duke Carl. His feelings of inadequacy even lead him to doubt his literary talent. But after reaching this low point in his self-esteem, his sense of direction asserts itself. With renewed faith in his ability, he resolves to continue his struggle as a poet and as a writer. A group of students now come to take him enthusiastically to Mannheim. The play ends on a high note of élan and exultation. Before taking leave, Schiller exclaims:

> Lend my your weapons for the task of deliverance,
> Lend me your fiery sword, oh poetry!
> . . . But I—off and away in storm and stress—
> The world my home, humanity my love! (28)

Notwithstanding these rousing lines, which by no means are devoid of poetic quality, Marie Ebner's other plays met with even less success than that encountered by her three historical dramas. Although she was judged gifted by some contemporaries, especially in the area of the social drama, few of her plays were printed, even fewer were performed. The negative reception of her plays caused her much grief. As a consequence she clutched at straws, interpreting Otto Ludwig's severe critique of the dramatic techniques of "Mister Eschenbach," by condemning their epigonal and imitative quality, as a kind of acknowledgment of talent. Had this great man not after all paid some heed to her dramatic efforts? Yet his judgment left little room for comfort. His limited recognition of her talent is overshadowed by critical remarks pointing in the opposite direction. He saw little of Schiller's greatness in Eschenbach's dramatic efforts, charging that wooden language and rhetorical prose had replaced the Classical poet's depth of thought and contents. In his view, Eschenbach's dramatic talent betrayed the influence of the Laube School and lacked all originality.[15]

There seems to be little doubt that Marie Ebner was deeply hurt by this criticism. The very fact that she later on refused to have her plays included in her collected works—a decision, by the way, which has been honored by all the editors of her literary oeuvre to the present day—is ample proof that she took very seriously Ludwig's critique and that of some of the local Viennese critics, who reviewed her plays performed in Vienna. Her three-act drama *Die Schauspielerin* (The Actress) did not even see the stage. Laube—at the time still director of the Burgtheater—rejected it when Ebner forwarded it to him in 1861. It deals with the exclusivity of the artistic calling, a theme which Grillparzer had successfully treated in his *Sappho*. The actress Helene Walter matures into a truly great female performer of tragedies only after getting over an intense but basically unhappy love affair.

A similar fate befell Marie Ebner's drama *Das Geständnis* (The Confession) in 1863, in which the Burgtheater actress Julie Rettich performed the leading role during provincial try-outs of the play. Marie Ebner became inspired to write it by a real happening in aristocratic circles of Vienna. A marriage enters the crisis state. A young woman is on the verge of submitting to the pleas of a suitor. When her old mother-in-law recognizes the danger to her son's happiness, she reveals her own past trespass to the young woman. It had led to an illicit love affair and caused immense feelings of inner guilt and pain to her while she was playing the role of an honored wife and mother in an unsuspecting family.

But Marie Ebner's love of satire and her sense of humor also led her to try her hand at social comedy. In the one-act play *Die Veilchen* (The Violets), the authoress humorously attacks "harmless" little social lies. Not surprisingly, the plot reveals unmistakable autobiographical references. The female protagonist, Countess Franziska, who loves violets, social contacts, and city life, is considerably younger than her husband, Count Sigismund Andlau. They are in many ways opposites. He loathes violets and her gossipy female social acquaintances. In the end she learns that nobody likes to hear the truth about himself. She loses, in fact, all her friends on account of her truthfulness. Now she and her husband can go back to their country estate. Her ultimate realization is: "What is the sense of staying if I can tell people only the truth?"[16] This comedy was performed eight times in the Burgtheater.

The frolicking dramatized novellas in one act, *Ohne Liebe* (Without Love) and *Bettelbriefe* (Begging Letters) were equally well received. *Ohne Liebe,* likewise containing auto-biographical details, was performed in the Berlin Residenz-Theater (Residence Theater). The young Countess Emma has been in love practically all her life with her cousin Marko. He, however, loved her like a brother and married her girlfriend. But now that the latter has passed away and he has become a widower, Emma and Marko can get married after all, provided that—as she insists—it is done "without love." Another concern of hers is revealed at this point: "I want to be your equal partner for life and in all things, which do not exceed my comprehension, your first resort."[17] He agrees to her conditions, taking her word for it. The punchline here is the author's clever retort to a popular saying berating the talkativeness of women: "A man—one word. / A woman a dictionary." Ebner wittily changes this disparaging adage to: "A woman—one word." (37)

But another comedy, *Männertreue* (Fidelity of Men), pat-terned after a novella by the Italian Renaissance writer Mat-teo Bandello, met with much more limited success. It was performed only a few times at the Böhmisches Landestheater (Bohemian Provincial Theater) in Prague after it was translat-ed into Czech by a Count Kolowrat. The one-act play *Die Selbstsüchtigen* (The Selfish Ones) was even less successful. After its first and only performance at the Vienna Stadt-theater (City Theater), the play was canceled because of un-favorable reviews. The Viennese theater critics of the day were, in effect, with only few exceptions very hostile to her productions. In retrospect, it seems that especially the Stadt-theater was a difficult forum for relative newcomers to the stage like Ebner-Eschenbach. This newly founded theater brought Heinrich Laube back to Vienna as its director in 1872, after he had been forced out of the Burgtheater in the previous decade and had subsequently gone to Germany to continue his career as a theater director there. The Stadttheater was planned from the very beginning as a bourgeois and liberal counterpart to the aristocratic and highly restrictive atmosphere of the Burgtheater. Its patrons, well-to-do members of the upsurging Viennese middle class, wanted to have their own theater and public forum to represent and display their newly gained wealth and social well-being. The competition with the Burgtheater for recognition was therefore stiff and few punches were spared in this not always fairly fought struggle for cultural preeminence in the city.

When Ebner completed her comedy *Das Waldfräulein* (The Forest Miss), in 1872, Laube wanted it shown in the Stadttheater. The comedy promised to be a special event, for rumor had it that Baroness Ebner-Eschenbach was about to present a play critical of the highest level of Austrian aristocracy. The play's initial performance at the Stadttheater on January 14, 1873, was heralded as a great social event. It was performed before an audience of well-to-do burghers filled with titillating expectations. Marie Ebner conceived the plot of *Das Waldfräulein* in 1861, the year of the Austro-Hungarian *Ausgleich.* Only a few years prior to this historic watershed a number of knowledgeable contemporaries—to mention Grillparzer and Palacky—prophesied the downfall of the bias toward and outright hatred of the empire's many minorities and the rise of the Slavic people in certain areas of the domain to new heights in the event of a political coalition between the German stock and the Hungarians. The author herself shared these views. Thus the principal character of the comedy, the backwoods baroness Sarah, may be looked upon as an emblematic figure and a symbolic representative of the young, unspent, and rising Slavic peoples in the monarchy.

This young and unspoiled aristocrat of Slavonic background—very much like Marie Dubsky— grew up close to nature. Her feelings and reactions were consequently natural. Moreover, because of her upbringing in the relative solitude of the countryside, she was without the social ills of Viennese society and especially its women, with whom she is forced to deal. Laube, in fact, on staging the play wanted to give it this inner meaning. An early impetus for Marie Ebner to write the play was Josef Christian von Zedlitz's epic poem *Das Waldfräulein*. She had been familiar with Zedlitz ever since her early formative years, when her husband to be, "Uncle" Moritz, introduced her to him. On first glance, Zedlitz's poem is both a poetic glorification of the Rhine and a tribute to the virtues of unspoiled womanhood. The young heroine grows up in the seclusion of the countryside. Unspoiled as she is, she differs greatly from her worldly contemporaries. Zedlitz pointed out in the preface of his epic what his deeper aim was:

> Not moral is every loathsome custom
> . . . .
> For only outwardly do you show moderation
> And call what is murky clean and what is clean
> murky.[18]

Clearly his main focus and concern was social criticism. He questioned the norms and ways of social behavior on the part of the vast majority of his contemporaries. This is in essence also Marie Ebner's mode of approach. As in Hugo von Hofmannsthal's later play *Der Schwierige* (The Difficult One),[19] there is much empty prattle in her comedy among society people who—and this is where her criticism set in—have little of substance to say to each other. But Marie Ebner's wit and her satirical vein are not directed at society as a whole but more specifically at the members of her own social class, the aristocracy. Her heroine is everything they are not: naive, yet smart, educated as well as outspoken. She has been brought to Vienna by her father to find a husband. But how will this be possible? The way she acts, nobody will be willing to marry her. Consequently, she has to be retrained, or so the members of her circle feel. She must become acculturated, so to speak, to the manner of her aristocratic peers. As the play unfolds, this proves to be impossible. She commits all sorts of *faux pas*, including the unforgivable one of talking with servants about her personal affairs. In addition, she misses no opportunity to be critical of her fellow aristocrats: "You are useless creatures in God's world, learning nothing, doing nothing, and laughing at those who learn and achieve something. . . ."[20] At the end, though, she finds a young man of her circle, Paul, who not only falls deeply in love with her and is willing to marry her, but whom she can also love and respect in return.

The question presents itself: why did Ebner's social comedy fail and with it her attempts to establish herself as a playwright? To be sure, the comedy was rather well received by the general public; but it was roughly treated by the press and by literary critics. The powers that be were evidently not eager to see a social satire of this sort on the stage, nor did they appear to be prepared to take the work of a woman playwright seriously. Hence it is no coincidence that this play, offensive as it appeared to be to influential sectors of Austrian society, led to a theater scandal at its first performance in the Stadttheater. The still powerful and dominant aristocracy did not appreciate this mirror image of itself. Just as obvious is the fact that the character of the "Waldfräulein" is autobiographical. Like Marie Ebner, the comedy's main character was argumentative, persistent, outspoken, socially abrasive, but still kind and filled with compassion for all who were deserving of it, especially those of the lower classes.

Marie Ebner, deeply hurt by the severity of the critiques and worn down by the many years of apparent futile struggle for public recognition, was emotionally, psychologically, and intellectually not prepared to continue writing drama. She resolved to give up writing for the theater and kept her word to the end. She had fought unsuccessfully for nearly thirty years to become a dramatist. Her failure was understandably a terrible blow to her authorial pride as one of her letters to Devrient confirms, in which she wrote: "Just as my poor hero, I should have been born fifty years ago if I would have wanted to achieve more than personal clarity, the capacity to come to grips with myself, or . . . the type of resignation which has nothing to do with utter pessimism."[21] Years later she was to write in a novella these very words of personal criticism. A critic, as the story line has it, incapable of great literary achievement himself, explains to a poet: "You have been born too late. Thirty or fifty years ago, people would have understood your aims. But today? The people for whom you are writing have died."[22]

It must be added, however, that Marie Ebner also had to deal with a formidable domestic critic over the years: her husband Moritz had told her already six years before her latest theatrical flop, after reading a number of critical revues of her previous dramatic productions: "You carry my name. I will not see it reviled in such a way."[23] There can be little doubt that her husband's displeasure with her unsuccessful dramatic efforts weighed very heavily on her mind and greatly influenced her decision to desist from pursuing any further endeavors along these lines.

Yet, all these critical voices notwithstanding, at least two of her dramas, *Maria Stuart in Schottland* and *Marie Roland,* as well as her comedy *Das Waldfräulein* deserve not only to be resurrected from literary oblivion as reading material, but merit also to be performed on the stage. These plays— stylistically dated, but still well executed—should not be regarded as forsaken and forgotten museum pieces of an earlier epoch. They offer historically valid social views and commentaries as well as timeless truths about the human condition as seen from the perspective of a socially aware and politically alert woman. What seems to be even more important about these plays in our own day, they are very entertaining.

Objectively speaking, though, the theater of her day, while still receptive to the style and ideals of the Classical and post-Classical periods, was much more open and eager to receive and try out new ideas. Moreover, the public as a whole wanted to see realistic plays with a flair for pressing contemporary problems. The theater critics, sensing the general trend, honed their pens in the same direction. They judged Marie Ebner's historic tragedies and her social plays inspired by dramas and dramatic techniques of Schiller, Grillparzer, and Bauernfeld passé. Moreover, in her social plays, which satisfied the taste of the general theater-going public, she was deemed to compete unsuccessfully with the popular French conversational comedies of the period. But this severe criticism, which led to such personal heartbreak for the author, was soon enough to turn into a boon for German and women's literature. It gave Marie Ebner the impetus to develop her literary talents in a different direction. Within a few years after her nearly total failure as an author, success came to her in another literary field. Almost miraculously, she was well on her way to becoming Austria's most popular narrative writer of the period.

Chapter III

STORIES TO TELL

What makes for a popular narrator? This question is as timeless as it is difficult to answer. Because of her husband's concern over her past failures as a writer and her own seemingly uncontrollable passion to continue writing at all cost, Marie Ebner was keenly interested in finding an answer. What raises the level of difficulty of the query is the powerful argument that popularity and excellence in the arts, just as in the political and social spheres, can rarely, if ever, be equated. But, then again, who is to say for sure? Can the democratic process or, put into language more conducive to the arts, the proverbial will, if not taste, of the public at large be readily and easily dismissed as immaterial? Is the age-old notion of *vox populi, vox dei* nothing but a social fairy tale?

To be sure, the canon of successful popular writers, perennially enshrined in the public mind, goes back to the very roots of all civilizations that ever developed the skill and power of script and writing for public consumption. It all seems to have to do with the innate gift, if not genius, of a writer to tell the kind of stories that will capture and fascinate the human imagination. The contribution of women in this endeavor should not be underrated. Even generally acknowledged antifeminist cultures, as, for example, the Arabic one, pay tribute to a woman's gift for story telling. Thus Scheherazade, who is traditionally credited with being the narrator of the *Arabian Tales of a Thousand and One Nights,* must have surely been thought of as a powerful, fascinating, and ingenious storyteller, inasmuch as by relating her tales to her sultan husband over a thousand and one nights she was —as the story frame has it—capable of keeping him from his intention of killing her.

Marie Ebner was obviously in no danger of meeting such a dire fate, but just as surely her stories must have been judged to be very good by the male editors and publishers of her day not to have met with rejection, which for her—still feeling the pain of her failure as a dramatist—would have been the equivalent of artistic and intellectual oblivion, if not death. Moreover, her stories and novellas were—her *Prinzessin von Banalien* (Princess of Banalia) and the later volume *Parabeln, Märchen und Gedichte* (Parables, Fairy Tales, and Poems) notwithstanding—no fairy tales of a freewheeling imagination that was carried off on the wings of folklore and popular superstitions. They were to some extent laced with poetic and even romantic motifs of a bygone era. But in essence they were conceived in the realist spirit of the age in and for which they were written. They also reflect in an unmistakable manner the intellectual, psychological, spiritual, social, political as well as philosophical backgrounds and beliefs of the author. Their topics and themes are manifold and vary from portraying the bucolic life in the country to the depiction of a number of succinct shades of the social life in the city. There are further variants within these parameters, which result in the contrasting and blending of demographic and sociological features. Class structures are frequently exposed, and differences in life styles are expounded. The propertied and the proletarians, society's rich and poor, the mighty and the humble are presented to the reader on this broad canvas. Marie Ebner focuses on people—a carryover from her beginnings as a dramatist—rather than on background descriptions and nature scenes. In the geographic sense, her stories sweep the western and eastern landscapes of the Empire to some extent but concentrate principally on the people of Moravia and Vienna. This approach leads to a heavy focus on the Slavic and German element in the multi-ethnic Austro-Hungarian populace. But frequently, the conditions of minorities, as for example the Jews, are also considered.

Viewed along generic lines, her stories could be grouped into those tales approaching almost novel length and complexity—such as *Jakob Szela* or *Der Kreisphysikus* (The District Physician), exposing life and conditions in the eastern province of Galicia—and into shorter ones with narrower focus, which could be categorized as novellas or even short stories. Examples of the latter categories are *Die Spitzin* (The Female Pomeranian Dog), ascribing human behavior to an animal and vice versa, or *Ein Lied* (A Song) with its concentration on a dying child. These tales, moreover, are homespun and based on some prior vicarious experience, if not outright autobiographical recollections, such as *Die erste Beichte* (The First Confession). They lead into the proverbial "kleine Welt" (small world of the petite and petty bourgeoisie) of the early Faustian experience or are sociocritical exposés of the "grosse Welt" (grand world of the upper classes) of the Austrian nobility of which she herself was a member. Of the latter, two antithetical tales, *Komtesse Muschi* (Countess Muschi) and *Komtesse Paula* (Countess Paula), serve as examples. In *Die Freiherren von Gemperlein* (Barons of Gemperlein) Marie Ebner created a tale that blended outright humor and ever so gentle social criticism into a unified whole. It should also not be overlooked that the author interwove practically all of her stories with pronounced dramatic elements, which should not be surprising considering her previous and—in the very early stages of her narrative writing—her simultaneous experiments in the dramatic genre.

However, no matter how hard one tries to categorize Marie Ebner's shorter narratives by convenient labels, one is thwarted not only by her epic versatility and multiplicity of themes, but also by her refusal to identify or even distinguish in some of her narratives among *Geschichte* (story), *Erzählung* (larger story), *Novelle* (novella), and *Roman (novel)*. Yet in so doing, she was—if one considers the practices of some of her older contemporaries, most notably the Austrian master story teller Adalbert Stifter—not all that unique in avoiding such—to her—artificial distinctions. Of special interest also is her broad epic mood, which extends from the humorous and comic via the satirical and sociocritical all the way to the melancholy and tragic. Here, too, as in her dramas, she is beholden to some extent to epic models, principally the Russian writer Turgenev, but also to Franz Grillparzer. All in all, she could even be called a romantic realist because many of her plots involve love stories. But just as in the social sphere of her stories, her concept of love does not include romantic elements alone or any such interludes between men and women in isolation. Rather it encompasses the love of a parent and a child, or that of siblings for one another, the loving devotion of servants toward their masters and mistresses, the *agape* and loving kindness that certain individuals practice in their dealings with their fellow human beings, and it even extends beyond the human sphere into the animal kingdom, relating the universal and almost mystical power of this seemingly all-pervasive force. In one of her aphorisms she makes clear that love of humankind and the motherly instinct of necessity go hand in hand: "Love all people, but make the one who suffers your child."[1]

The titles that Marie Ebner gave to many of her stories and collections of tales and novellas reveal to some extent their contents, plots, themes, and social backgrounds. A case in point is her very first venture into the epic genre, *Aus*

Franzensbad: Sechs Briefe von keinem Propheten (From Franzensbad: Six Epistles By No Prophet, 1858), the title of which reveals not only the satirical content of the piece, but also points to its personal, if not autobiographical bent. The same could be said about *Die Prinzessin von Banalien* (The Princess of Banalia, 1872), which is regarded by many, including one of her earliest interpreters, the renowned literary critic August Sauer, as the actual beginning of her narrative writings. The author herself, however, sought distance from both works for understandable reasons. Doubting the book's merit from the very beginning, she had *Aus Franzensbad,* an attempted satire in epistolary form about the life of the upper classes in general and especially its female members, printed anonymously. Later in life she became convinced of its immaturity and expunged this early tale from her collected works. *Die Prinzessin von Banalien,* which Marie Ebner called "the fairy tale of blind love," attracted little attention. The main reason for this lack of appreciation lies in the fact that the work's plot did little to unveil the author's intentions. The romantic fairytale princess from the kingdom of banality must perish, it seems, because of her passion for the exceptionally handsome son of the wilderness, who, like nature itself, knows of no other fidelity but that to himself. The narrative can be read as a social satire about a banal world in which the sensitive female protagonist is by her inner make-up ill equipped to find fulfillment. However, it might also be interpreted as a fairy tale with more somber undertones. The princess, forced to live in a world ruled by heartless and domineering men, cannot find happiness in life and must therefore seek it in death. The complex symbolism of the tale lends itself to either interpretation. Thus the reader has difficulty to make up his mind whether he should laugh or cry about the outcome. The melodramatic elements of the story line veil the tale's intended message. The author had occasion to read her story in the house of Josephine Baroness von Knorr, another woman writer. Among the guests were her friend Betty Paoli, whom many called Grillparzer's "female Eckermann," Auguste von Littrow-Bischoff, and Ferdinand von Saar, with whom Ebner had been acquainted for the past five years. Yet even in this close circle of friends this story of a misguided love elicited little enthusiasm.[2]

The slim volume *Erzählungen* (Tales), however, which was printed by Cotta three years later in 1875, contains a literary gem, *Der Spätgeborene* (The One Born Late), which made both literary critics and reading public aware of her epic talent. In this story she utilizes for the first time a very personal theme: the tragic existence of the artist denied recognition. The author exposed in the novella her innermost feelings about her own past hopes of becoming a famous dramatist. Written from the heart by way of a catharsis, Marie Ebner presents in the story's idealistic protagonist the lowly government worker Andreas Muth, who writes plays, some of her own disappointing experiences. He is a lonely, modest, and impractical individual, comparable to Grillparzer's protagonist in *Der arme Spielmann* (The Poor Musician). Accustomed to receiving rejection slips from the theater directors to whom he sends his manuscripts, Andreas Muth is content reading his dramas to a sole listener. As his symbolic name suggests, he has the courage to go on, but he also seemingly lacks the forcefulness to make himself a success. As fate would have it, one of his plays is put on the stage by mistake with devastating results for his artistic ego. His contact with the outside world and its malicious criticism causes him to lose faith in his talent and eventually in himself, thereby threatening his continuing existence. Caught in the web of politics as well as in the destructive forces of an inimical press, he is totally crushed as a writer and as a person. Baroness von Knorr, who had continued her support of Marie Ebner, passed the manuscript of the novella on to Ferdinand von Saar for critical reading. It was Saar's approval of it which encouraged Ebner to offer it to Cotta.

Years later Marie Ebner attempted a psychological variation of the theme in *Der Spätgeborene* in another novella, which she titled *Verschollen* (Lost and Forgotten). Its central figure is an artist who has withdrawn from life and society, giving up his previously acquired fame in the process. His former student Heini Rufin, who has become a famous painter of modernist art, wants to enhance his artistic imagination by usurping his old teacher's ideas and passing them off as his own. But before he commits the contemplated plagiarism, he has to know whether the old master is still alive. He finds him in his secluded house in the mountains, where for all practical purposes he is dead to the outside world. While Andreas Muth portrays the artistic type who although immersed in life cannot cope with it—a state of mind which the old master also experienced earlier—the young and unprincipled Heini Rufin represents the type of a modernist artistic climber who is eager to succeed at any cost. However, he also embodies youth. The fate of the old, it seems, is to give ground to youth, one way or the other, so that new modes of doing things can ensue, even if they are morally questionable. This rather grim conclusion, based on observation and direct experience, is the author's acerbic critique on questionable artistic and social developments in her country. The world has a passion for change, but change for its own sake is not desirable. It is especially repugnant if it results in the co-opting of old ways by unscrupulous manipulators, leading to a mere window dressing of the old at the expense of moral rectitude. The theme of the artist *reductus,* a recurring topic and personal favorite of the author, is developed on a grand scale in her last novel, *Agave,* which I shall discuss in depth in the next chapter.

The collection *Erzählungen* contains four other tales of less philosophical portent. Of these, *Die erste Beichte* (The First Confession) is the most personal because of its autobiographical roots. It is the literary version of an occurrence in Marie Ebner's childhood which almost cost her her life. Having been told that it was better to die than to offend God with a sin, young Marie Dubsky took this admonition literally, and on feeling one day that she had committed a sin, she jumped out a window in order to kill herself. Fortunately, the attempt failed. She merely bloodied her head. *Die erste Beichte* is Ebner's first story drawn entirely from personal childhood experiences. In its replication of real life events, it confirms the old truism that life, though stranger at times than fiction, is still one of fiction's best sources.

Of the other tales the novella *Chlodwig* is a psychological study. It relates the psychic distress and collapse of an aristocrat who has been deceived by a cold and conniving woman who had hidden her true feelings for him. Although he experiences the disintegration of his persona, he is incapable of resisting the lure of the past. *Ein Edelmann* deals with the rights and duties of aristocracy. Because he married a bourgeois woman, Count Tannenberg forfeits his right of inheritance and assumes another name and identity. However, events force him to disclose his past to his son. Marie Ebner gives the story a sociopolitical slant. The aristocracy has lost its right to existence, its *raison d'être*. by neglecting to employ its energies for socially useful tasks and goals. The clock of progress cannot be turned back. When economic distress forces the protagonist to pursue a bourgeois career, such as becoming a merchant or an industrialist, his aristocratic moorings become irrelevant. Ultimately, the only way left open to him is to become a farmer. Even though he is aware that choice might lead to his financial ruin, he still admonishes his son to continue the pursuit of worthwhile goals no matter how great the struggle may be. In stark contrast to the idealist message and setting of the tale, the novella *Die Grossmutter* shows abject social misery. It is based on the experience of a doctor friend who became privy to the plight of an old woman. This relatively short story introduces another central theme in Ebner's narrations: the plight of the underprivileged classes. In this novella, the focus is on the suffering of an old woman, who in many small ways carries features of the author's own beloved grandmother but, alas, is ravaged by poverty because of social neglect. Marie Ebner contributed substantial sums later in life to assuage the plight that impoverished women faced in old age.

In terms of their reception by the public, these tales—as her publishers began to notice with chagrin—appeared to fare as badly after their publication as her dramas had done on stage. Yet Marie Ebner continued to write more narratives as if she were under a spell of compulsion. After completing her first novel *Božena* in 1876—a work which will be analyzed in detail in the next chapter—she ventured into describing a world of which she had relatively little knowledge. It was the milieu of Viennese socialites and hedonists. She named the story—which was completed in 1878 but published thirteen years later in 1891—*Margarete*. This popular female name is encountered frequently also as the designation of a common European meadow flower, generally referred to as "daisy" in the United States. However, it may relate as well to a variety of single-flowered chrysanthemums, especially the *Chrysanthemum frutescens* of the Canary Islands. The term is of French origin and can be traced back to the Middle French "margarite," meaning pearl, but also daisy. The principal female character after whom this story is named is the personification of all these meanings and more. She is exquisite but also common, beautiful but also obnoxious, loving but also hateful. Above all else, she is driven by overpowering passions and appears mentally deranged. The story also reveals her past. She is the daughter of a wealthy factory owner. Her fortune changed after her father's death. She lost her mother a few years later. Neglected by her stepfather, she went to Vienna, fell in love with a sculptor, who left her for another woman after fathering her child. She dearly loves her illegitimate son Georg, but tragically he is run over by a carriage and dies as a result. Her frantic pleadings to God are in vain: "Why should I?—A misfortune?—Why did it strike the innocent child and why me?—Haven't I suffered enough? I don't want to suffer anymore! I am willing to fight! I won't let my child go, won't let him die! I'll breathe life into him. I'll share my life with him. I have enough for two!" (Hafis, 8:309).

The owner of the carriage that killed the boy is Count Steinau. In trying to make amends he falls passionately in love with the grieving mother, who, however, favors his younger friend Robert. Full of passion herself, she goes as far as attacking and wounding Robert with a knife when he rejects her advances. Eventually she surrenders to Steinau's pleadings and becomes his mistress. They live together in an illicit relationship, unperturbed by the gossip the liaison elicits in aristocratic circles. Robert, though happily married, is coaxed by friends to attend a masked ball of loose morals, presided over by Margarete in the guise of Cleopatra. In the process of their renewed encounter he succumbs to her ravishing and bewitching beauty and guile. But soon after this passionate night, Margarete becomes severely depressed. She kills herself at the grave of her son on the very day on which he was born. She could no longer bear to live a life of empty debauchery.

Despite its melodramatic ending, the story has a modern flair to it. Doubtless it is Marie Ebner's most passionate tale. On the other hand, however, it is also the most hopeless and base depiction of womanhood which the authoress ever attempted. Still, this psychological tale of sin and expiation, madness and guile, perverted love and lust reflects a great amount of her sympathy for the maddened heroine. who stumbled and fell to such depths of depravity because of an unkind fate and an inner need to compensate for the love she craved but never received, neither from her parents, from a man, nor tragically, even from her child. Marie Ebner had serious doubts at first about this story, fearing that its sexual exposés might lead to accusations of lewdness. Moreover, she also experienced difficulties finding an appropriate publisher. She consequently delayed its publication and even refused to have it included in the first edition of collected works.

In 1879 *Die Freiherren von Gemperlein,* a work of an entirely different mood, appeared in the periodical *Die Dioskuren* (The Dioscuri). The themes of passionate love and debauchery gave way to the kind of humor heretofore rarely encountered in women's literature. Although it was in its thematic focus also a psychological tale dealing with the human urge to love and to procreate, the emphasis of this novella points in other directions. Marie Ebner pokes fun at her own social class, the aristocracy, thereby giving the plot some sociopolitical overtones. The underlying motif of the story is not even fictitious; the old country aristocracy was indeed dying out. But the author presented the lighter side of this basically tragic process. Just as Marie Ebner had intended it, the novella left the reader smiling, if not laughing, instead of having him cry in empathetic sentimentality. The misbegotten amorous affairs of the two country squires were highly praised by Paul Heyse, one of the era's most famous German writers of novellas. He, in fact, included *Die Freiherren von Gemperlein* in his collection of novellas, *Neuer Deutscher Novellenschatz* (New Collection of German Novellas) and thus gave the still largely unknown Ebner much-needed exposure.[3] The noble, though constantly quarreling brothers, with their innate urge for love, are perfect opposites, threatening to go their different ways. One is a conservative, the other a radical. They never share the same opinion and are always fighting with each other. Even the reading of the newspaper leads to disagreements: "Suddenly one could hear the one or the other shout: 'Oh, these asses!" and a newspaper was thrown under the table. That was the customary beginning of a political debate. Usually it ensued and concluded in about fifteen minutes with the mutual remark: 'Go to hell!" (Hafis, 3:242-243). Although they quarrel endlessly with one another they stay together. As their lifelong quest to get married and to continue their family line comes to naught, they do not become misanthropes or quaint old cranks. Nor will they leave each other. In their innermost being they are kind, compassionate, and noble human beings, who show much concern and even love for each other when put to the test. Despite their rough edges they practice the meaning of *noblesse oblige* in their dealings with others and in so doing represent the best that Austrian country aristocracy had to offer. With obvious reference to her own earlier experiences in Zdislawitz, Marie Ebner shows the positive aspects of living in a quiet country setting and the beneficial results for the inner lives of the brothers: "The great imagination with which nature had endowed them developed in the quiet Wlastowitz much more abundantly than would have been possible in the turmoil of city life and brought them a lot of pure joy. . . ." (246).

These positive features notwithstanding, *Die Freiherren von Gemperlein* is ultimately a tale of resignation. Such stories are almost endemic in the literature of Poetic Realism. Ebner's novella was republished in the volume *Neue Erzählungen* (New Tales, 1881). Of the other narratives included in this collection, one is of special interest. Entitled *Lotti, die*

Uhrmacherin (Lotti, the Clock Maker). It relates the meeting of skilled artisanship and literary life in Vienna in the novella's two principal characters. Julius Rodenberg, a writer who published many of Marie Ebner's stories, had brought it out independently in the previous year in his *Deutsche Rundschau* (German Forum). Ebner had sent him the manuscript of the novella on December 10, 1879, and had received a favorable, highly complimentary reply and acceptance from Rodenberg six days later. The work was to appear in the March 1880 edition of his prestigious magazine. This highly coveted exposure was a first giant step on the part of the author toward national recognition. It opened the doors of other publishers for her narratives throughout Germany. She had begun her correspondence with Rodenberg five years earlier in 1875. After many letters their first personal meeting was to occur in March 1880 on the occasion of a guest lecture by the author/publisher at the literary society Concordia. Marie Ebner was introduced to Rodenberg by an old friend of hers and her husband's, the president of the society, Joseph von Weilen. A cloud developed on the silver lining of their relationship on July 23, 1881, when Rodenberg rejected the manuscript of her *Margarete* as unsuitable for his magazine. This rejection was perhaps the primary reason why Marie Ebner withheld this novella from publication for a full decade. Only then, at the height of her fame and with the onset of a much more liberal social climate, did she resubmit it to Fritz Mauthner for his *Magazin für die Literatur* (Magazine for Literature), not withholding Rodenberg's earlier rejection, however. As regards Rodenberg's personal feelings toward her, he was to confide in later years of their professional relationship that among his most renowned contributors—Keller, Heyse, Storm, Louise von François—Marie von Ebner-Eschenbach was the easiest to deal with. Eventually, their professional relationship was to develop into genuine friendship. In the course of the years, Rodenberg published some of her most successive narratives in his *Deutsche Rundschau*. Among them were: *Die Totenwacht* (Death Watch), *Mašlans Frau* (Mazlan's Wife), *Glaubenslos?* (Without Faith?), *Rittenmeister Brand* (Cavalry Captain Brand), *Verschollen* (Lost and Forgotten), *Der Erstgeborene* (The First-Born), *Der Vorzugsschüler* (The Honor Student), and *Der Einbruch* (The Break-In). Rodenberg's magazine also featured Ebner's childhood recollections *Meine Kinderjahre*. His diary of April 23, 1896, shows the following entry: "The most beautiful hours, on Monday afternoon, we spent in the old house of the Ebner-Eschenbachs, Rothenturmstrasse 27—so old that the over eighty-year-old lieutenant general spent his childhood there from the age of seven. . . ."[4] In 1897, Marie Ebner dedicated her collection of stories, *Alte Schule* (Old School), to Julius Rodenberg. He returned her compliment in 1907 in his idyll, *Aus der Kindheit* (From One's Childhood), "the most endearing book of Rodenberg" according to Anton Bettelheim.[5] The author/publisher treasured his friendship with Marie Ebner to his dying day. He considered her in addition to Gottfried Keller and Conrad Ferdinand Meyer to be one of his greatest contributors.

Lotti, die Uhrmacherin, the first of her stories which Rodenberg published, is by no means one of her best. The plot appears somewhat contrived. Lotti, daughter of an old Viennese watchmaker and a practitioner of the art of watchmaking herself, was betrothed in past years to a promising poet of aristocratic background. Spoiled by lavish praise, he jettisons his ideals and, after Lotti steps out of his life, becomes a fashionable and shallow writer of sensationalistic tales. Generous beyond measure, Lotti helps her former fiancé, when he is down on his luck, by selling her greatest personal joy and treasure, her precious collection of watches, and turning over the proceeds to him. Materially poor now, she has

enriched herself through caritas and purity of heart. Ultimately, the aging spinster finds happiness by the side of a like-
minded man of her own social class. It is the inherent social
theme rather than the tear-jerking quality of the story line
which the modern reader may still find interesting. A considerable part of the Austrian aristocracy of the second half of
the nineteenth century relied, because of their lavish and
wasteful life style, on the rising bourgeoisie to replenish their
vanishing fortunes.

Much more modern, because of its timeless psychological
depth, is the novella *Nach dem Tode* (After Death), also included in *Neue Erzählungen*. A widower, who has shown
little appreciation of and love for his deceased wife, is about
to begin a new marriage in great haste. Only then does he
come to realize his irretrievable loss. One is reminded on
reading this tale of one of the famous sayings of Confucius
regarding the three ways open to us for attaining wisdom.
One is through the power of thinking and its corollary insight, which is the noblest way. The second is through imita-
tion, the most common path. The third one, however, is that
of experience, easily the most bitter of the three. The story's
protagonist, Count Paul Sonnenberg, has followed the third
way. But not all is lost. He becomes aware of the superficial
nature of the woman with whom he fell in love and whom he
wanted to marry: "Foolishness has once upon a time led to
the statement that love was blind and thoughtlessness me-
chanically repeated it. This is not true. Love has a penetrating
eye for the smallest flaw of the beloved . . ." (Hafis, 3:350-
351). Ultimately he breaks off his relationship with her and
resolves to honor his deceased wife's love for him and her
memory by living with and for his daughter Marie, her true
legacy: "The heavenly gift of love comes to us just once:
only once—and never again" (371).

The plot and the very name of the daughter of the story's

principal character point to autobiographical connections and to the uneasy feelings Marie Ebner still harbored for her own father, who had gone in the opposite direction. The novella, moreover, conveys significant political observations in its framework: "Austria stood at that time at the brink of an abyss to which its policies had led it: the strife of the nationalities was ablaze internally while life and death struggles threatened from without" (308-309). Ebner also crafted a political mouthpiece in this novella, Baron Kamnitzky, who is highly critical of the upper classes and their lack of appreciation of the country's problems:

> I mean all of you: political scientists, rejuvenators, reformers of the state, builders . . . indeed noble builders: . . . Filling in one crack in the wall, doing repair work on the roof, and do not notice . . . that the foundation walls are cracking. . . . Do you know what the foundation is called, on which alone a firm edifice of state can be built? Sense of justice. Exactly, what we don't have. . . . You are making laws? You are just wasting your time! We have enough laws, but the people who are supposed to obey them, they haven't been born yet. . . . The laws emanate from the state, which is our enemy, devouring every single one of us as Ugolino devoured his children. . . . (374).

In addition to these themes, which in retrospect sound prophetic, the author began to develop a focus that was to evolve into a major topic in her oeuvre in later years: a special interest in and love for animals:

> Why, they don't deserve this attention, these graceful black horses with these beautiful heads, these slender necks, these pliant pastern-joints. Their silken hair is

as black as the night and its splendor rivals that of
moonlight. They stomp the ground with artful grace
and playfully inflate their nostrils, as though they felt
that the eye of an aficionado were focused on them.
. . . (318).

In 1883 Marie Ebner published some of her later most beloved novellas in a collection to which she gave the appropriate title *Dorf- und Schlossgeschichten* (Tales of the Village
and the Manor). Among these, *Krambambuli,* the story of a
dog torn in its allegiance between two masters, is doubtless
her most popular narrative. Inasmuch as the tale's main character is an animal and not a human being, it is also one of
the most unique stories conceived in German literature up to
this time. A regional gamekeeper by the name of Hopp buys
a purebred hunting dog from an alcoholic vagabond for
twelve bottles of cherry brandy. He develops such an obses-
sion for the animal, named Krambambuli, that he even
neglects his wife. The author introduces this theme in philosophical terms: "Man shows an interest in all kinds of things
and creatures. Genuine, everlasting love he experiences—if
at all—but once" (Hafis, 4:117).

Hopp makes the dog his closest companion. Obedient and
faithful beyond belief, Krambambuli joyfully returns to
Hopp, even though badly battered, after the latter was
ordered to give the beautiful dog to his employer, the count.
The animal prefers to die rather than stay with the count. In-
evitably and tragically, however, the dog does not pass the
most difficult of all possible tests of loyalty in the eyes of his
new master. The gamekeeper is ordered to track down a
poacher, who during his illegal hunting activities has shot
and killed the chief forester. It soon turns out that this criminal is none other than Krambambuli's former owner. When

the two can confront each other in a mortal shoot-out, Krambambuli inadvertently saves Hopp's life by jumping on the
poacher. Surely, he did not do it to defend his new master.
His action was an expression of joy at having found his old
master again. Hopp is able to take advantage of this situation,
He shoots and kills the criminal. But feeling that the dog betrayed him, he turns away from the animal. In an unforgiving
mood he lets Krambambuli starve at his door rather than ad-
mitting the creature back in his house and life.

The plot of this novella points to Marie Ebner's dramatic
beginnings. Its tragic protagonist, however, is not a human
but an animal that loses its life because of its inability to
serve two masters. In essence, the author indicts both of
them. The poacher is after all a criminal and murderer. Yet
Hopp also acts in an inhumane and murderous way. He treats
the dog like a personal slave in an unforgiving and unyield-
ing manner. He does not care at all about the animal's inner
life and feelings. Inasmuch as his action causes the dog's
death, the author condemns him too at the end. However,
there is another strand woven into the fabric of the story line
that is equally significant. It reveals the dog's inner life, his
psychic makeup. Surely, it is too narrow a view and does injustice to the narrative skill of the author to ascribe mere
human qualities to the animal and let it go at that. Recent
animal psychology has confirmed what Marie Ebner knew
over a hundred years ago through observation. A well bred
dog, like any other animal, has an uncanny ability to sense
human emotions and intentions and atunes his own actions
accordingly. He is not only man's best friend, but also man's
most astute observer. Fidelity to his master is second nature
to him, having been bred into him for countless generations.
Hence the tragic dilemma facing a dog caught between two
masters is real and innate, it is anchored in the psychic sub-
stratum of the species rather than being that of an animal

character to whom anthropomorphic characteristics have been ascribed.

Marie Ebner's profound interest in the psyche of animals led her to write two other remarkable animal tales later in life: *Die Spitzin,* which became part of her novella collection *Aus Spätherbsttagen* (From Late Autumn Days, 1901), and *Der Fink* (The Finch), included in the volume *Alte Schule* (Old School, 1897). In both novellas, however, the author changes her emphasis somewhat. They do not focus on the inner turmoil in the animal's psyche, as is the case in *Krambambuli,* but show how animals can affect and even change human lives. *Der Fink* tells the story of a young girl by the name of Pia who, on finding an injured young finch, intends to protect the little bird from a dog and a cat, whose instincts drive them to kill the bird. The girl is a half orphan who visualizes the bird's joy on finding its mother again, a feeling she herself was never able to experience directly. In addition to containing much autobiographical detail, the story carries an important message regarding the relationship between man and the creatures of the animal kingdom: "Human beings have a different vision and a different sense of responsibility" (Hafis, 10:28). The narrative also reveals the author's remarkable ability to enter the mind of a child and to expose the complex mechanism of a child's imagination.

Yet *Die Spitzin* proves that Marie Ebner did not completely abandon her earlier efforts of probing into the depths of the animal soul, especially on the theme of interaction between an animal and a human being. It is the story of an old female dog, a young boy—easily the poorest of the poor— and a profound change of heart. When gypsies come to a village in upper Austria and quietly depart in the middle of the night, they steal nothing to everyone's amazement, but leave a naked blond boy behind. The child is given the name Provi Friedhof. Everybody soon develops nothing but hatred for him, and the villagers even beat him whenever the fancy strikes them. He is treated in an especially cruel manner by the despotic man for whom he is forced to work. Clad in rags and treated worse than an animal, he passionately hates the inhabitants of the village in return. His only playmates are five wild boys in the neighborhood who have made animal abuse one of their main pursuits in life. They have especially mistreated a small female Pomeranian dog, resulting in the crippling of the animal. So severe were the dog's injuries that she is left with only three legs and one eye. To make matters worse for the animal, the boys have also regularly taken her litters away from her and drowned most of her offspring in the nearby lake. When the dog whines all night on one such occasion, looking for her young ones, Provi, who is forced to sleep in a small shed next to the dog house, becomes angry for lack of sleep and gravely wounds the animal in a temper tantrum. However, when he awakens the next morning, the dying animal brings him and entrusts thereby to his care her only surviving puppy before passing away. The author describes his reaction and his inner feelings in detail:

> 'Yea, yea!—You've been a mom!' . . . Overcome by the God-given pain of compassion and by sobbing, the boy started to writhe on the ground and cried for the old Pomeranian dog and cried for the tiny thing she left behind, which pressed itself against the mother's body whining for hunger and seeking nourishment at the fountain of life, which flowed so sparingly in the past and has now completely dried up. (Hafis, 5:274).

To obtain food for the puppy he does something he has previously refused to do for himself: he begs the innkeeper's wife for milk.   The most striking part of this animal tale in purely human terms is the profound change in the boy's mind and character after the dog's death. It is brought about by the boy's chance encounter with the motherly love of an animal. An innately desired, but heretofore never directly experienced awareness of the meaning of this natural force in human terms wells up in him and changes his personality. Although this transformation does not alter his lowly social status, his realization of the power of a mother's love releases by vicarious means not only pent-up feelings in him that cause him to cry, but also chastens and humanizes him. The story reveals in addition the fierce prejudice toward and outright hatred of gypsies among simple country folk in German-speaking lands. In the meantime more than a century of unprecedented social and political upheavals has gone by in Central Europe since Marie Ebner wrote *Die Spitzin*, yet there has been little change of heart toward gypsies in those parts, as recent events have confirmed.

In two of her *Dorf- und Schlossgeschichten, Der Kreisphysikus* and *Jakob Szela*, the author returns in part to an earlier love and interest: history. But whereas in her dramas her historic topics came from western sources, the locale and action of these two narratives unfold in the east: in Galicia. The action in both novellas takes place in the Galicia of the midforties of the nineteenth century. This was the time of the peasant uprisings in this part of the Austrian empire. The critic August Sauer referred to both novellas as strictly historic.[6] They describe the misery of peasant life in an age that can be characterized most charitably as patriarchal. Sauer conjectured that the author, who never visited these areas of the empire, may have obtained some of her insights from stories and political confidences that her husband shared with her.

Der Kreisphysikus is the story of a double conversion. As Anton Bettelheim, another early critic of Marie Ebner's writ-

ings, observed: "The contrast of these fates develops within
the inner core of Jewish and Slavic traditions."[7] The novella
relates, in effect, the transformation of the local Jewish
physician Nathanael Rosenzweig from an egotistical individual interested primarily in amassing personal wealth to a
person who dedicates his mental and physical energies to the
welfare of the masses in an apotheosis of socialist ideals,
which the author fully embraced. Her idealism leads this
narrative to the proximity of the contemporary Russian
writer, philosopher, and mystic Tolstoi. Nathanael Rosenzweig has had a difficult childhood and knows the meaning
of deprivation. Consequently, he has fought hard all his life
to advance himself and attempt to gain riches. Still, he enjoys
an excellent reputation in the prerevolutionary Galicia, where
he pursues his career as a physician. His view of the peasant's lot is clinically sympathetic:

> . . . the peasant is dumb. But how is he going to be-
> come smart if, by chance, he has not been born that
> way? Of course, the peasant is lazy. But how would
> diligence benefit him? It would never get him any-
> where. His diligence would benefit his master more
> than him. Surely, the peasant takes the money he has
> earned today to the tavern right away. But his waste-
> fulness comes from his misery. Misery is not thrifty.
> Misery is incapable of fathoming a thought as fruitful
> as that of becoming thrifty. (Hafis, 4:46-47)

However, after meeting the Polish idealist Eduard Dembowski, he undergoes a nearly miraculous, complete transformation of heart and spirit. The latter, an aristocrat, gave up all
his wealth to become a messenger of love and compassion
for the poor. The Jewish physician follows his lead. When
the Polish nationalists rise against the Austrian rule and

hegemony in these parts, Dembowski joins them, without, however, giving up his basic fight of helping above all the poor and oppressed. Nonetheless, the Austrian authorities pursue him, seeing in him only a dangerous political rabble-rouser. Nathanael can save him only with difficulty. When Dembowski disappears from public view, rumor has it that he died as a political martyr. In reality, as Nathanael later discovers, he lives on not as a revolutionary leader but as a peasant with wife and children who works for the good of humanity on a daily basis. In Nathanael he has found a genuine and worthy disciple.

This novella shows both an interesting parallel and a pronounced contrast to Adalbert Stifter's *Abdias*. In both novellas the protagonists are Jews cast in the traditional mold of nineteenth-century public awareness. But, whereas Stifter's Abdias does not undergo any substantial character transformation in the denouement of the story, the change in Ebner's Nathanael Rosenzweig is profound. Again, in contrast to the Jewish reception of *Abdias,* which was essentially negative, *Der Kreisphysikus* met with approval in Jewish circles. Two leading Jewish literary critics, Ludwig Geiger and Ludwig Philippson, praised the author for her complete lack of religious prejudice and for her literary artistry. Philippson wrote in 1884 in *Die allgemeine Zeitung des Judentums* (The General Jewish Observer), one of the leading Jewish periodicals of the period: "The authoress displays a high degree of artistry in portraying people and situations realistically and of imbuing them nevertheless with idealistic tendencies and features. We consider this to be the greatest display of novelistic art."[8] Ultimately, Nathanael Rosenzweig can be viewed as a character in which Jewish ethics is fused with Christian *agape,* genuine humanism, and idealistic socialism into a unified whole.

Jakob Szela, Marie Ebner's other revolutionary tale in her

Dorf- und Schlossgeschichten, bears witness to her strong belief that the unsettled conditions leading to the anti-Austrian revolt were the result of the social misery of the peasants. They were cruelly exploited by the Polish nobility, who owned the land in the countryside and were kept in a state of total dependency. This, Ebner felt, was also the reason why the peasants, who were usually of Ukrainian stock in eastern Galacia and ethnic Poles in the western parts, did not want to join the aims of Polish nationalism, for the abuse of the Polish landowners was much worse than that of the Austrian officials. However, the Polish peasant leader Jakob Szela occupies a middle ground in the conflict between the aristocratic Polish nationalists and the Habsburg regime. He protects the peasant community from the excesses of the Polish nobles and is reluctant to join ranks with the latter in their fight against the Austrian crown, since the oppressed peasants see no need in ousting the Austrians who give them some legal protection. On the other hand, he also saves the endangered offspring of a Polish nobleman from the justified wrath of the peasants. This action leads to controversy:

> Some call Jakob Szela a leader of the people. Others refer to him as a person leading the people astray. The first group sees in him a model of 'beautiful loyalty.' The second one regards him as a robber and a destructive lunatic. . . . Rarely were there such diverse opinions about a historic personality as was the case with the Galician peasant Jakob Szela, tiller of land at Smarzowa in the vicinity of Tarnow (Hafis 4:86).

In the end, he is attacked and reviled by all.

Thus Marie Ebner's portrayal of Jakob Szela aims to achieve some balance. To be sure, the final verdict on this controversial historic figure and on the peasant revolt he led is still not in and may never be fully attainable. Too many national interests—chiefly those of Austria, Poland, and Ukraine—are still entwined with the past blood letting of the historic revolt and counterrevolt in midnineteenth-century Galicia. Franzos—who was a native son of the region and of Jewish origin and wrote extensively as a journalist, sociopolitical analyst, and writer of imaginative literature about the area—fully shared Ebner's view of the principal culpability of the Polish landowners in the plight of the impoverished and abused peasant class. He, too, had little sympathy for the Polish nationalists, whose foremost aim it was to resurrect an independent Poland, which as the result of three successive partitions in the later part of the eighteenth century had lost its national identity.

Jakob Szela has been called a Michael Kohlhaas of the East. This historical protagonist of Heinrich von Kleist's most famous novella by the same name was an honest and law-abiding German horse trader of the sixteenth century, who, because of a terrible wrong done to him, turns into a fierce avenger and regional scourge. Szela is also a historic contemporary of Franzos's Taras Barabola, the central character of the latter's novel, *Ein Kampf ums Recht* (For the Right).[9] Barabola, similar to Szela, leads a peasant revolt in the Carpathian mountainous region of the Austrian empire prior to 1848. By contrast, however, his insurrection is directed against the Austrians. Parallel to Franzos's treatment of the theme and contrary to Kleist's heroic figure, Szela does not fight the established order for personal reasons but for the welfare of the peasant community. Yet the outcome is similarly tragic.

The sociocritical novella *Er lasst die Hand küssen* (He Sends a Hand Kiss), the principal story of Marie Ebner's sequel collection *Neue Dorf- und Schlossgeschichten* (New Tales from the Village and the Manor, 1886), also deals with the fate of oppressed people. The inner core of this frame-type story takes the reader back to the past, while the frame itself establishes in a satirical way some reference to the contemporary scene. The plot unfolds in the castle of a wealthy female landowner, who listens reluctantly to the tale of an old aristocratic admirer of hers about his grandmother's dealings with a disobedient subservient. He relates without regrets or any kind of scruples how aristocratic highhandedness cloaked in an air of false morality ruins the lives of two simple people, that of her gardener Mischka and of his love. The tenderhearted woman, in fact, succumbs to death on being treated too harshly, and Mischka is beaten to death for lack of subordination. The mistress's pardon comes too late. Breathlessly, her servant reports to her at the end: "He sends a hand kiss, but he has already died" (Hafis, 4:277). Some analysts and literary historians miss Marie Ebner's intended subtlety and render the story's title incorrectly by providing the missing *Umlaut* (modified vowel) in "lasst." The apparent grammatical mistake and the resulting spelling error are by no means an oversight on Ebner's part. They are an intended reflection of the level of German used by the less educated and disadvantaged lower socio-economic element of the populace. The simultaneously critical and moving effects of the story are skillfully revealed. Thus Marie Ebner unmasks both the cruel feudal practices of aristocratic landowners and their shallow and hypocritical morality. This novella is an especially apt vehicle of reflecting the social history of the declining Habsburg empire as a whole and of simultaneously revealing the unjust treatment and inhumane conditions to which the lower classes and its servant element were subjected.

Sauer and other critics have pointed out that many of Ebner's stories take place in the highest circles of the Austrian aristocracy or show members of the lower classes in their dealings with this privileged group.[10] Such is the case in *Wieder die Alte* (The Same Woman Again), the lead story in the collection *Miterlebtes* (Tales of Experience). A woman teacher by the name of Claire who, in order to repay a family debt, is forced to serve as a governess and a lady companion in the dreary household of a count brings the family sunshine and cheer. An unhappy love affair temporarily unbalances her sunny disposition. But soon enough she heroically overcomes her state of depression and becomes "the same woman again" —as the title of the story puts it—that she had been before. In her basic portrayal Claire appears to be a sister of Lotti, the watchmaker. She is no longer young, is poor and lonely. Yet her capacity to serve and entertain others and her cheerfulness make her a superb companion in "high society" where people are bored and spiritually hollow. When Claire appears changed because of a man's infidelity, her "slippage" is noted by her aristocratic employers with indignation. But when she recovers her previous disposition, they gleefully observe that she has become herself again.

A companion story in the same collection, *Die Kapitalistinnen* (The Woman Capitalists), takes a turn toward the outright humorous. It is a Viennese tale about two elderly sisters, both spinsters, who appear to be related to the Gemperlein brothers. Though equally peculiar, their basic concern is not the continuation of their lineage but survival in the here and now. To this end they need to harness their limited capital reserves. The author relates quite humorously how their modest savings cause them a series of mishaps and a great deal of unwelcome excitement. This novella could also be seen as a social satire on nineteenth-century capitalist practices and on the way in which the lower middle class is exploited by the monied establishment.

By contrast, *Ein kleiner Roman* (A Short Novel) is a very serious narrative. Helene, a cultured and sensitive young woman, is employed as a governess in the house of a count. Her principal task is to tutor and supervise his daughter Anka. Helene is cast in the mold of Claire. Like the woman teacher in *Wieder die Alte* she is a member of a lower social class and consequently subjected to abuse and exploitation. Structurally a frame-type story, though, the inner theme of the narrative is also more expansive. In addition to the general theme of contrast between the nobility and the bourgeoisie, the juxtaposition of aristocratic master and lower-class servant is explored. The count falls in love with Helene after she helps him when he needs support. Up to this point, he, a widower, has lived solely in a world of his own recollections, memories and make-believe: "The faith in the love and faithfulness of his wife cast a bright spell over his recollections. The faith in the goodness of his child shone with gentle radiance over his entire life" (Hafis, 9:280). Yet, in reality, his daughter Anka is spoiled, selfish, and incapable of returning or even feeling love. This lack of feelings on her part leads to constant frictions with Helene. It is obvious that Anka stands between Helene and the count, who wants to marry her. Helene feels compelled to decline his proposal after a heroic struggle with her conscience. In view of the frictions between her and her present ward and prospective stepdaughter Anka, she has no other choice. In the end, she feels obliged to leave permanently, never to see the count or Anka again. In the outer frame of the novella, Ebner, in her early sixties now, creates a remarkable aged role model, perhaps even an attempted self–portrait projected into the not all that distant future:

> The *Hofrätin*[11] is a charming, beautiful, indeed an extremely beautiful, woman in her seventies. It would be difficult to imagine more aristocratic features than those of her delicate snowy-white face covered with

countless wrinkles. The large, light-brown eyes have
lost their fire a long time ago, but they radiate an
inner light, a spirit filled with kindness, intellect, and
nobility. Her lips have become pale and narrow. Yet,
irrespective whether they are silent or move in speech,
they convey an expression which one best calls
lovely. (229)

In 1892, one year after Marie Ebner's *Margarete* was finally published and three years after the publication of *Ein
kleiner Roman,* her volume *Drei Novellen* (Three Novellas)
appeared in print. The most outstanding of these is *Oversberg: Aus dem Tagebuch des Volontärs Ferdinand Binder*
(Oversberg: From the Diary of the Apprentice Ferdinand
Binder). It is the latter fictional character, in fact, who—
though intellectually limited—writes the story of the novella's protagonist, while another story character, the inspector,
relates it somewhat excitedly. Marie Ebner's use of two nar-
rators creates the unique artistic effect of this tale. Both are
part, moreover, of a lively group of men who meet and remi-
nisce about the remarkable Albrecht Oversberg in whom they
see "a simple and noble human being" (Hafis, 10:157). He
was never able to marry the woman he loved, yet he still
helped to take care of her child after she passed away. It is
both his simplicity and his nobility of heart which make him
the male counterpart of Marie Ebner's earlier character
Claire. His nobility of spirit is also reflected in his symbolic
name.

A novella dealing essentially with characters of opposite
nature is *Das Schädliche* (1894). The author presents here by
way of an autobiographical memoir the sad story of a husband and father who seeks true love but experiences the
seamy side of it in the two women in his life he truly cares
for, his wife and his daughter. They are both very attractive

women and consequently attract men. But they lack the capacity to return genuine feelings. It is obvious that they are mentally deranged. Thus Edith, the narrator's wife, professes prior to leaving him: "If you cannot love me any more like that, I'll be lost. I have too small a soul, I believe, and too little heart, I know. . . . Give me your soul, your heart in order that I'll be alive again" (Hafis, 5:37). Although doing his best to raise his daughter Lore in the hope that she might fill the void he experienced over the loss of his wife, who died after she left him, he fails. Lore turns out to be as driven and deranged as her mother was. His desperate struggle for her soul is in vain. She has the psychological makeup of a predator. The regional hunters call carnivora who feed on useful animals "the pernicious," which carries the connotation of evil itself. When Lore is ultimately shot by a jilted and jealous lover, the father, concerned at first, decides to let fate take its course. " She lives to the detriment of anyone who comes close to her. She is noxiousness in persona. Let's do away with all that is harmful in the world. Let fate take its course! Let it happen!" (76).

The author depicted two women in this novella, mother and daughter, who are cast in an opposite mold to Goethe's uplifting model of the eternal feminine leading humanity onward and upward. Just like her female protagonist in *Margarete,* both Edith and Lore exemplify the depravity and moral abyss into which womanhood can descend. This negative portrayal is far removed from earlier Classical and post–Classical models that inspired Ebner in most of her other works. Her character depiction in this narrative is affected by contemporary Naturalist theory of heredity. Evil is shown to result from unfavorable heredity factors which even careful and loving social grooming cannot overcome.

Die Totenwacht (Death Watch, 1894) is a novella that borders on the modern short story. Another modernistic fea-

ture of this narrative is the use of dialect, a stylistic feature
of literary Naturalism. The dialogue form employed, however, points back to Marie Ebner's earlier dramatic writing.
There is, in effect, very little traditional narration. The plot
focuses on Anna, the story's main character. She is still a
beautiful woman, although marked by years of hard work.
Now she stands death watch at the bier of an old woman in
the poorest hovel in a Marchfeld village. The well-to-do
peasant farmer Georg Huber joins her. The conversation that
ensues between them reveals the past. It is the story of sexual
abuse and rape of the then young girl by Georg. The result
of this crime led to Anna's pregnancy and motherhood. Although she loved and accepted the illegitimate child, it died.
At this stage in her life, she cannot forgive Georg, despite his
change of heart and his willingness to marry her now, years
after his criminal trespass. The past is more than prologue in
this story. It is present in the eeriness of the death watch and
it casts a deadly shadow over any possible reconciliation between Anna and Georg and any successful attempts of recon-
sideration and rectification. It appears that the author wants
to convey a strong moral point: rape is a crime against the
sanctity of womanhood that is unforgivable.

The year 1896 saw the publication of two more of Marie
Ebner's narratives that found favor with readers and critics
alike: *Rittmeister Brand* and *Bertram Vogelweid.* The first is
essentially a story of deglorification of the military, which
theme is also its sociocritical feature. The plot's principal
character, Dietrich Brand, comes from a long line of merchants, but, because the pursuit of a military career appeals
to him, he bolts the family tradition and becomes an officer.
An idealist at heart, he lets no opportunity pass him by to
praise the military for its potential to do good:

. . . Dietrich dealt with his favorite theme with special

> warmth: No institution is so well equipped and so
> capable of fulfilling the great task of educating man as
> the institution of the armed services. It makes the
> highest demands on love of duty, integrity, and valor
> (Hafis, 7:213).

Soon enough, however, he begins to realize the limitations of this profession and the true way of life it represents.
Having lost Sophie, the woman he loved in younger years to
a competitor for her favors, he becomes a witness to the
unhappy passion his younger comrade Wildenstein develops
for the temperamental Hungarian wife of his commanding
officer, Count Prach. The latter, overcome by jealousy,
conspires to force Wildenstein into suicide. Brand sees no
other recourse to rectify this crime and to punish its perpetra-
tor, Count Prach, for having stooped to such behavior than to
leave the military. He intends to challenge the colonel in
duel. Although suffering wounds himself in the duel, he
succeeds in wounding Prach so severely that the latter is
forced into retirement. Brand, however, has become so dis-
enchanted with military life and its amoral ways, based as it
seems solely on a command structure bound to lead to moral
abuse, that he will not permit anyone to address him as "Captain" anymore—a common practice in Austrian society to
show respect not only for present achievements but also those
of the past. But rather than becoming embittered with life, he
now helps Sophie, who has become impoverished, and her
children. Thus he will be able to conclude his life as a
Samaritan and humanitarian, after having been a fighter for
morality and justice in his younger years. Doubtless Marie
Ebner was inspired in her conception of this noble and heroic
figure by the character and professional experience of her
husband Moritz, whose own somewhat premature and hastily
arranged retirement from the military—although never fully

disclosed in all of its ramifications—found measured reflection in this narrative. The tale also contains autobiographical references regarding her own life. At one point in the story the author has Brand express her own thoughts about the lack of children of one's own in a person's life:

> One finds the best remedy for overcoming the pain of not having children of one's own by extending one's love to those of other people. Embrace the children of others, Madame. As for me, I intend to take care of the children of my deceased friend (246).

In the same year of 1896, *Bertram Vogelweid* was introduced to the reading public. It is a humorous and slightly satirical tale about the harried life of a writer and journalist as well as the precociousness and lack of common sense prevalent in aristocratic circles. With regard to the first theme the contemporary reader might have had little difficulty in recognizing in the novella's central character the—at the time—well-known writer, journalist, and publisher Karl Emil Franzos, with whom Ebner entertained friendly professional relations for decades. Viewed from this perspective, the novella is a story a clèf and a humorous parody of the busy and frantic life of this Austro-Jewish author. Like Franzos, Bertram is a writer and an editor of a large paper. He is slightly balding, visibly aging, and hates his job, which his mother has suggested to him. The day does not have enough hours. Editorials, human interest stories, two novels simultaneously for publication in serial form, all of these are in a day's work:

> The fruits of his insane diligence are lying on his desk. Four surveys, four cultural commentaries, the final installments—that indeed he had promised him-

self solemnly—of his last novels: of his folksy novel
with its ideal anarchist, its capitalist exploiters; of the
barons, counts, and princes living off the blood and
sweat of the common folk; of the novel of high
society with its ambiguities, its risqué dialogues.
Extremely imitative of French models, yet in all its
parts nothing but champagne changed into beer.
(Hafis, 10:217)[12]

Moreover, his conscience bothers him. Occasionally, he has
to reject writers and poets, whose works he has not even had
the time to read. On the verge of a nervous breakdown he
decides to go on a vacation. But as fate has it in this satire
with serious undertones, instead of finding much-needed rest
and relaxation at the country estate of his aristocratic friends,
he is overwhelmed by a swarm of literary enthusiasts and
amateur writers and poets, who turn his hunger for escape
from work into more mental stress. The only relief comes
from Gertrud, with whom he falls in love and whom he will
marry. She is one of those whose poems he had rejected
without even having glanced at them. Now he can make up
for these past sins. On the more serious side in this prepon-
derantly funny story are two statements interspersed in the
novella's lively dialogues and interchanges. The first, regarding the Germans, has uncannily prophetic qualities: "To be
sure, even the Germans give in if they have no other choice"
(268). The second remark deals with Austria's political future
and the role that socialism might eventually play in the
country:

We are moving toward a new social order. The next
step toward this goal is called the solution to all
economic problems, and it lies, so they say, in the
nationalization of everything. Now, my nonexpert

opinion is that the transition to this broad avenue of salvation will lead us again on to the narrow paths of the past such as, for example, home industry (318).

Marie Ebner prophesies here in a very humorous way not only a bit of socioeconomic development in the future of her own country but also in that of much of the world.

Marie Ebner's self-proclaimed *Altersdichtung* (writings of old age) begins with her book *Alte Schule* (Old School). Next to the animal story *Der Fink,* the artist tale *Verschollen* holds the greatest promise for the modern reader. The young, un-principled painter Heini Rufin attempts to perfect his art under the tutelage of an older, once well-known painter and professor. This overly strict taskmaster withdrew from society years ago in order to devote himself more fully to the memory of his deceased wife, a beautiful and noble woman. He had wronged her, for, as he learned too late, he failed to grasp the full depth of her love and devotion. At the end of the story it is doubtful or at least it remains unresolved whether Heini has profited from the old man's experience. He seems, after all, more interested in co-opting the old master's artistic ideas than in learning how to become a better balanced human being. The story's inner theme of belated awareness of missed opportunity to personal happi-ness and fulfillment closely resembles that in Marie Ebner's earlier novella *Nach dem Tode,* which, however, has a more positive and satisfying conclusion.

In 1898, also marking the death of her husband Moritz, Marie Ebner completed and published a frame–story entitled *Die arme Kleine* (The Poor Little Girl). It is actually the story of the Von Kosel family, into which as the youngest of four children Angelika is born. Her older three brothers are all of gigantic proportions. When her mother sees her after birth, she exclaims: "You poor little girl" (Hafis, 6:10). This reference to her in a non-pejorative sense takes on a life of its own even after the mother passes away prematurely. True to her mother's prediction, Elika, as she is called, really develops into a frail, sickly child and young woman. Her father, who was grief-stricken at first after her mother's passing away, soon marries again.

The title of the narrative and its early focus on Elika are misleading to some extent. The tale's main plot soon revolves around Luise, the young and beautiful aunt of the Kosel children by second marriage. One of them, Josef, falls seriously in love with her. The story also highlights a young neighbor named Levin, who, after causing much social upheaval in the placid and conservative rural community, returns to Australia from whence he has come on a visit to the old country estate of his parents. Interwoven with these story lines is a strong focus on the suffering of the lower classes. The main spokesman of this theme is Heideschmied, the sympathetic old tutor of the Kosel children. He advises Josef, the socially most astute member of the Kosel clan, that the plight of poor city folk is worse than that of the underprivileged in the countryside because of overcrowding. Although the ending of the story is deliberately vague and left open, there are hints of a positive and negative outcome. Elika, who will most likely die prematurely, as her mother did, has matured emotionally and intellectually beyond her age. She is of great comfort to her brother Josef and helps him to overcome his disappointment over his unrequited love for Luise. The latter has followed Levin's call and invitation to join him in Australia. It is left to reader's imagination to envisage that life in this distant and largely unknown continent will be freer and better for them than in their old homeland.

Marie Ebner's next collection *Aus Spätherbsttagen* (From the Days of Late Autumn, 1901) proved to herself and the world that, though a septuagenarian now, her powers as a storyteller were undiminished. In addition to the animal tale *Die Spitzin,* two other narratives in this collection are outstanding: *Der Vorzugsschüler* and *Mašlans Frau.* The first is a tragic story of a hard-working but by no means brilliant student who is pushed by his father, a lower government official of modest means and background, to achieve in school beyond his capacity. Georg Pfanner has been an honor student in the gymnasium. Hard work, determination, and his mother's loving understanding and support, on the one hand, and his father's stern prompting, on the other, have made this goal possible for him. His father, a lowly railroad official, is a typical parent of the time: dictatorial in his demands, expecting and getting utmost respect and total obedience. Although his ambition for his son is vicarious, he is in his own way not an unloving father. He wants his son to be valedictorian of his class so that the doors of social success would open up to him one day. To move the boy toward this goal, he does not shy away from giving him an occasional beating.

Georg, partly out of fear and in part out of a sense of obedience, forces himself to succeed in his studies. His secret love, however, is music. This one-sided father and son conflict, remarkable for its psychological depth and timeless modernity, must take its predestined course to the predictable tragic ending. When Georg fails in his attempt to remain class *primus* because of competition from an intellectually superior student, he sees no other recourse but to commit suicide by drowning himself in the Danube. The outcome of this story provides its own indictment of a basically flawed family structure and a social system so inflexible that its victims are hopelessly caught in its web. Still, the author does not conclude this tragic novella by pointing accusing fingers. She has Georg's mother find the strength of heart and of character to forgive her equally devastated husband:

"You only wanted to do what was best for him" (Hafis, 5:148).

This narrative in which a mother's selfless love for son and husband plays a crucial role, is equaled in psychological intensity by *Mašlans Frau,* a love story that is at the same time also a tale of the tragic relationship between a husband and wife. The miller Matěj Mašlan is dying, but, as the local priest who is to give him the last rites learns with consternation, his wife Evi appears to have no compassion for the dying man. The local physician relates to the priest in this frame–type novella how this rift between husband and wife came about. Matěj, a dashing man attractive to women and attracted to them, simply could not keep his marriage vows. Evi, on the other hand, a faithful wife to him, lost one child after the other in childbed, a circumstance which did not help their relationship. When she discovered his repeated infidelities, she locked him out of their house. Seething with anger, Matěj vowed never to set foot in the house again. Evi, in turn, swore that she would also refrain from seeing her husband. Both kept their vows. Evi turned a deaf ear to the admonition of a male neighbor: ". . . you are not to take any vows. You just have to obey, and your husband has the right to command. That is how the law is written" (Hafis, 5:166). Evi and Matěj never spoke to each other again. Even though they still love one another after all these many years, the local priest's attempts to bring about a reconciliation between them are in vain. Only after her husband's death, when the neighbors bring his corpse home, does Evi reconcile with him. Although Marie Ebner's sympathies are basically with the woman, the story, inspired by Turgenev's style, shows the devastating psychological effects of pride and stubbornness on the part of both husband and wife. Their unwillingness to forgive and their strong, unbending wills destroy their marriage and their lives. The importance which Ebner attached to this theme is confirmed by the fact that she wrote two other novellas—*Der gute Mond* (The Good Moon) and *Uneröffnet zu verbrennen* (To Be Burned Unopened)—in which she also portrayed tragic marriages resulting from human weaknesses and shortcomings.

However, there is a second, more hidden theme in this story which is of equal importance to the author. It is highlighted by the widely held assumption of Marie Ebner's contemporaries that woman is inferior to man and that her lower status is codified by sacred law. This notion is based on the Lord's word to Eve in Genesis 3:9: "I shall greatly multiply thy pain and thy travail; in pain thou shalt bring forth children; and thy desire shall be to thy husband, and he shall rule over thee." Marie Ebner labored all her adult life to overcome the emotional and intellectual affects of these words. Seen in this context, it also seems only natural that the author called her female protagonist in *Mažlans Frau* Evi.

Two further novellas, *Der Erstgeborene* (The First–Born) and *Ihr Beruf* (Her Profession) were published in 1905 under the title *Die unbesiegbare Macht* (The Undefeatable Force). Both works deal with the power of love, which is shown as an unstoppable force of nature. It will assert itself no matter how great the obstacles may be. In *Der Erstgeborene* the central theme is the love of the simple peasant woman Ilona for her first-born son. She bore him out of wedlock to a count and was forced to give him up to the aristocratic father, who had taken advantage of her and had abused her sexually in her youth when she lived and worked on his estate. His stable boy Stephan, who married Ilona later, tried in vain to avenge her honor. Many years have passed, but Ilona, though happily married to Stephan and mother of two healthy sons fathered by him, cannot forget her first–born child, who has been raised in the count's motherless household. She feels sad and guilty thinking about him "He grows up in splendor, surrounded by riches, and is still poor" (Hafis, 7:74). When Ilona sees her first-born son again during a festival in the local castle, he also recognizes her as his mother. Their longing for each other was mutual. The author's message is unmistakable: no human force can nor should keep a mother from her natural child or vice versa. Mother and son will never be separated again: "The best that two human beings can owe to each other is exemplified by this mother and this son" (95). This homiletic conclusion of the novella reflects Marie Ebner's innermost beliefs.

The powerful theme of motherly and filial love is varied in *Ihr Beruf.* In this novella a young doctor named Forster falls in love with Johanna, one of Judge Staudenheim's five daughters. Although Johanna is also fond of the young man, she nonetheless spurns his advances because of his unconventional religious views which border on atheism. They ultimately separate. Forster goes abroad and Johanna follows her own religious calling and becomes a nun. Years later, she receives a letter from Forster, in which the dying man beseeches her to take care of his daughter after his death. When the girl, who speaks and understands only Spanish, arrives from overseas, she is frightened to death on seeing Johanna's black attire. The latter rids herself of it and resolves to forsake her calling as a nun and to become a caring foster-mother to the child of the only man she ever loved.

This novella betrays Marie Ebner's belief that faith in God, no matter how sincere, and complete dedication to His calling in the isolation of a nunnery are subordinate to caring for a child in need of a mother. Good deeds are more important than mere faith. While the author upholds this Catholic tenet, she simultaneously rejects the Catholic notion of performing the good deed of serving God in isolation. Loving kindness and care of others are social tasks that must be practiced in an extramural public setting, outside the confines of a convent, in order to be fully effective. Motherhood, however, is still the highest calling for a woman. It goes beyond giving birth to a child. The author shares the modern conviction that nurture is more significant in child rearing than nature.

In her next collection of novellas and short stories, *Genrebilder* (Genre Pictures, 1910), the author again turns for the most part toward the lighter side of life. The lead story *Ob spät, ob früh* (Whether Late or Early) is a light-hearted parallel to Turgenev's much more serious fare as presented in the latter's novel *Smoke* (1867), which captures the atmosphere of the famous spa of Baden-Baden and his novella *First Love* (1860), in which a sensitive youth falls unhappily in love with a playful young woman. The nineteenth–century Russian novelist and dramatist Ivan Turgenev (1818-1893), although producing a nationalist literature, was one of the most widely respected and influential writers of his age. While writing in the classical style of the earlier Pushkin, he anticipated European Impressionism. Although pessimism and nihilism overshadowed his worldview, his major novels, *Fathers and Sons* (1862), *Smoke*, and *Virgin Soil* (1877) were much admired. Equally influential were his many novellas, which contained the subtle artistry and brooding melancholy distinguishing his novels, but were also masterpieces of psychological analysis. All his major works became soon available in German translations and influenced Marie Ebner stylistically and thematically.

Ob spät, ob früh combines the setting of *Smoke* with the theme of *First Love*. But the tone is light and humorous. It relates the first amorous awakening of a young aristocratic chap who, on visiting a spa with his mother, becomes enamored of a mature woman there. Although the latter is highly flattered, she does not return his affection. One day in the future, he will not only love again but be loved in return.

Marie Ebner took the title of her story from the poem of Hermann von Gilm, quoting it as a motto and word of introduction:

And as late as it happened to you, you fiery
  yellow one.
Love stole its way into my heart and soul.
Whether late or early, it is all but one
Pleasure and the same painful dole. (Hafis, 9:7)

This short novella, doubtless also based on one of Marie Ebner's personal experiences in such settings, reads like a belated and slightly nostalgic sequel to her first attempt at narration: *Aus Franzensbad*. *Fritzens Ball*, however, is a downright humorous tale appearing in the same collection. Intermingled with mild social criticism, the story offers a satirical glimpse into the mostly wasteful and slightly boring aristocratic life in the moribund Austro-Hungarian monarchy, in which marriages between older men and younger women, illicit love affairs, intrigues, and entertainments of various sorts dispelled the emptiness of their lives. Fritz, the upstart son of a wealthy bourgeois industrialist, fits well into these circles.

The equally humorous tale *Unverbesserlich* (Incorrigible) takes the reader in the opposite direction. Life among the common people in the countryside is examined under the magnifying glass of mild social criticism. As it turns out, not Edinik, the black sheep of the village, is incorrigible but the villagers themselves, who are caught in the web of their own narrow-mindedness and prejudice. In spite of his ill repute as village "devil" and his mischievous behavior, he proves to be well-meaning. The village dwellers, on the other hand, are unforgiving and morally ossified. Even the two "good" souls in the community, the parson and his sister, are powerless to change anything. They want to continue living and functioning there and can ill afford to turn the villagers against them. Ultimately, they are forced to give in to the public demand to ostracize the young man. Thus, in this tale, village *Realpolitik* wins out over Christian *agape* and social consciousness.

The novella *Unverbesserlich* confirms that Marie Ebner was, albeit in a subtle way, still one of the foremost social critics among her writing peers. The tale's humor and its sarcastic tone cannot mask the author's underlying social concerns. It would therefore be incorrect to categorize her simply as a female representative of late Poetic Realism, a label quite frequently attached to her. Surely she does not share the proclivity of the majority of her male literary contemporaries toward—what has been called—*Resignation,* a tendency of period writers to withhold political or social commentary for fear of dire repercussions. Although this anguish on the part of German and Austrian writers was less germane after the Revolution of 1848, which overthrew the dreaded Metternich regime with its feared censorship, genuine freedom of speech and thought was still not permitted in German-speaking lands in the second half of the nineteenth and well into the twentieth century. Switzerland was the only exception to this pattern, but even there only one author of renown, Gottfried Keller (1819–1890), took full advantage of these freedoms in such narratives as *Das Fähnlein der sieben Aufrechten* (The Banner of the Upright Seven) and *Martin Salander.* Writers like Marie Ebner labored under a twofold handicap. By background, marriage, and social status she belonged to the highest circle of Austrian society, the privileged aristocracy. As a writer she had to be cautious not to offend her husband and her immediate family in a blatant manner. She could not afford to be overly outspoken or offensive in her public pronouncements. To be sure, she was both by nature and by her upbringing incapable of assuming the role of a literary or political radical. In the second instance she was a woman. Her gender was undoubtedly even a bigger drawback. Her early training, as well as contemporary mores, severely proscribing what might have been tolerated in males, simply forbade her to engage in acerbic verbal attacks on social and political ills. Still, she was too astute an observer of her society and too steadfast in her beliefs to fall silent. She consequently tended to engage in social criticism of a less direct and severe nature in much of her writings and to use more cautious and veiled means to denounce the social and political evils she saw. This tendency as well as her well tempered humor are, however, also the hallmark of a wise, nearly classical approach to one's dealings with life and are not alien to—what could be called—the Austrian mind.

Stille Welt (Quiet World) is Marie Ebner's last collection of tales, published one year before her death. *Der Herr Hofrat* (The Privy Councillor), the lead story, reflects to some extent her preoccupation with her recollections of Grillparzer, which appeared in print a few months later. Hofrat Hügel, the story's central character, is a kind old man, a retired government official who, like Grillparzer, lives out his life in the protected security and care afforded him in his Vienna apartment and his Mödling villa by a well-meaning woman who looks after his physical needs. He surrounds himself with like-minded friends and even plays host to a distant young relative and his young bride. The outside world with its social issues and problems is excluded for the most part, exerting little influence on the Hofrat's idyllic lifestyle. Only occasionally is reference made to illness and death. Marie Ebner's own situation and her feelings toward the outside world in the waning days of her life are also reflected, as the following quotation from the narrative makes clear:

> Gone! Gone! The theater as an artistic experience, as
> a place for growth of the upper and lower classes, is
> dead. There are tragedies, but there is no longer a
> tragedy, nor a drama, only actors . . . and the public
> is ever so much closer to the lowest common denomi-
> nator than the highest . . . a bunch of rabble. . . . The
> poetic element has been swept out of the tragedy, the
> music eliminated from the opera. Instead, there is
> noise, the louder, the better . . . (Hafis, 6:229–230).

Favorable references are made to Heine's *Buch der Lieder*
(Book of Songs) and to Betty Paoli's verses with the intent
of conjuring up powerful images of true poetry from the past.
But Ebner does not permit herself to become mired in *Alters-
pessimismus* (pessimism of old age). The story ends with a
glowing account of youth and the author's optimism for the
future. The young couple leaves the Hofrat "with a bright,
sunny heart into a bright, sunny day . . . ; and thanks to their
love and enthusiasm, the world belonged to them" (2:72).

Marie Ebner's shorter narratives, written over nearly six
decades, and consisting of novellas, short stories, and sketches, reflect not only the growth and development of her own
skills as a popular storyteller, but also provide a nearly perfect mirror image of the broad scope of her literary interests
and her personal philosophy. Moreover, they offer as well an
accurate record of her social and political concerns and beliefs as they evolved over these many years of her life. Her
stories amused and horrified, surprised and shocked the reading public of her day. Some of them are, as we have seen,
incredibly funny. The majority of her tales, however, betray
her dramatic origins and her proclivity toward dramatic, if
not tragic, events and outcomes. They are about conditions
and people in the cities and in the countryside, in the villages
of her native Moravia and its castles. Occasionally, they also

expand into the eastern territories of Austro-Hungary. They deal with the rich and powerful as well as with the poor and dispossessed. They tell about aristocrats and the common people, masters and servants, and in a moral sense also about the good, the bad, and the indifferent. Husbands and wives, parents and children are shown in ingenious plots of confrontation and harmony. Remarkable is the fact that she also wrote tales about animals that exceeded their earlier anthropomorphic use in fables long before such stories became popular in German literature. Most of all, however, her shorter stories concern love and reason. We will next determine whether her longer narratives conform to these patterns or, if at all, transcend them.

Chapter IV

THE NOVELISTIC WORKS

Marie Ebner's foray into novel-writing began in a somewhat haphazard fashion. It was a natural extension in her general development as a fiction writer, a probing, so to speak, of new dimensions in heretofore untried territories of plot construction, rather than the outcome of deliberate planning. For one thing, she herself never referred to any of her longer narratives as novels per se. To be sure, in this reluctance—at least as far as Austro-German letters were concerned—she was in excellent company. Adalbert Stifter, Austria's foremost prose writer and older native role model for Ebner, also refrained from calling his two longest narrations, *Nachsommer* (Late Summer) and *Witiko,* novels. Although they are generally acclaimed today as representing the greatest novelistic achievements of the age of Poetic Realism, he called them *Erzählungen*, which in German carries the much less imposing connotation of *tales.* Marie Ebner followed suit, also referring to her more extended narrations in this way.

Even though her lack of precision has not affected the favorable reception and the popularity of the majority of these works among her readers, it has caused some uncertainty, if not grief, among her interpreters and analysts over the many decades since they were written and published. Only three of the five works which I am about to discuss in this chapter have been generally designated as novels and have been treated as such in extensive philological studies in recent years. Earlier investigations of her oeuvre, principally that of Johannes Klein, added a number of other epic works of hers to the list of Ebner-Eschenbach novels. This uncertainty in the classification of some of her works is noteworthy. It points to problem areas beyond her oeuvre and reflects a recognizable lack of focus and cohesion, clarity and development in the novel genre as such in much of earlier German literature.

As Georg Lukács—one of the foremost theoreticians of the novel—had occasion to point out in a seminal study, the evolution of the novel in the literature of the German-speaking peoples is complex and in some ways parallels their history.[1] The term *Roman* used in German to describe or discuss this literary form, the very word, in short, affixed to it, is of non-German origin. It stems from French usage dating back to the twelfth century, which referred to works not written in Latin but in the local vernacular, the so-called *lingua romana,* as *romans.* It mattered little whether such works were composed in verse or in prose. The term soon spread to the German-speaking lands. Thus contemporaries there called the courtly verse epics of Hartmann von Aue, Wolfram von Eschenbach, and Gottfried von Strassburg[2] *romans* after the French model. Only with the onset of the eighteenth century did the idea set in that novels should be literary prose works, a notion that is universally accepted today.

By and large, however, the acceptance of the novel in German lands as serious literature, in which one could express noble ideas and uplifting ideals rather than just telling adventurous, amorous, and entertaining stories of low literary quality, was slow in developing. The generally acknowledged breakthrough in public perception, putting the novel on an equal footing with other literary genres such as poetry and the drama, occurred with Goethe's *Wilhelm Meisters Lehrjahre* (Wilhelm Meister's Apprenticeship Years) published in 1795-1796. This work was highly lauded, even celebrated, by the writers of early Romanticism and led them to consider the novel as the best literary vehicle to encompass and reflect their love for artistic and intellectual universalism. The great admiration of these writers for *Wilhelm Meisters Lehrjahre* was further enhanced by the fact that it showed in form and content the development of the protagonist from a lower to a higher level of awareness and intellectual growth or *Bildung*. Still, as in other cultural and social areas, the evolution of the novel to universally accepted norms lagged behind in Germany throughout the nineteenth century, inadvertently aided by the fact that Goethe's and Schiller's efforts toward a nationally accepted drama—preceded by those of Lessing and supported by Hegel's weighty philosophical pronouncements—were such that the dramatic genre was considered to be the highest literary form of the age. This, in turn, led many of the contemporary writers to strive to establish themselves as dramatists. Marie Ebner's earlier efforts were by no means an exception in this undertaking. Other even more renowned writers of the period, such as Gottfried Keller and Conrad Ferdinand Meyer—to name two very prominent ones—also tried in vain to develop into successful dramatists. In addition, it must be said that—in the epic genre—with few notable exceptions, principally Stifter and Keller, the writers of Poetic Realism lacked the epic imagination and skill to write full-fledged novels equaling the literary works of their English, French, and Russian contemporaries.

Marie Ebner's situation was especially unique, aside from the fact that she was a woman writer. Inasmuch as both her literary love and her literary beginnings were in the drama, she transferred the temperament and technique of the dramatist from the very beginning of her career as a narrative writer to her narrative style. She never completely abandoned her inclination to have her plots evolve along dramatic rather than strictly epic lines. It was only natural for her to write her narrations in this manner. This, however, meant in turn that her plots tend to be largely straightforward, poignant, and compact rather than being diffuse, loose, and multifaceted. Her depictions of backgrounds, both social and natural, are to the point and convey the essentials. They lack to a great extent the broad brush stroke of epic canvassing and effusion. Her narratives avoid verbosity, a trait which has been traditionally and prejudicially associated with women. Ebner is not a writer of *epische Breite* (epic breadth). These factors help to explain why most of her narrations tend to be rather short and why she failed to designate even her longer ones as novels. She preferred the German term *Erzählungen,* which as a literary subgenre occupies in traditional German epic writing the middle ground between the *Roman* with its aim of showing the full development of an individual—such as in the *Bildungsroman* (novel of personal growth through experience and education)—of portraying broad historic backgrounds and developments—as in the *Geschichtsroman* (historic novel)—or of depicting a comprehensive social canvass—as in the *Gesellschaftsroman* (society novel)—and the *Novelle* (novella), which according to Goethe's classical definition—much expanded later, but never fully eclipsed—revolved around "eine unerhörte, sich ereignete Begebenheit" (an unusual past event). Her reluctance to designate her longer epic works as novels may also be partly explained by her modesty, which after the great disappointment of her first forays into the public limelight as a writer of drama became second nature to her.

Haphazard as Marie Ebner's entry into the novel genre may have been, it was not devoid of an awareness of the difficulties inherent in its evolution and the need for clarifying and improving its status, much discussed in her close circle of literary friends. *Božena* (1876), generally acknowledged as Marie Ebner's first contribution to the novel genre, shows some of the results of these fruitful deliberations. Held together by its principal character, the Czech servant woman Božena, whose name also provides the work's title, the novel is nonetheless not a typical German *Bildungsroman* or a related *Entwicklungsroman* (developmental novel) with an atypical female protagonist. For one thing, there is no real character development or growth toward a higher goal. Since the plot depicts the dealings of the main character with three generations of the bourgeois family Heissenstein, the novel could be designated as a *Familienroman* (family novel) or even a *Generationenroman* (novel of generations). In the latter definition it is highly innovative, for it was published a quarter of a century earlier than Thomas Mann's much admired and imitated trend-setter in this subgenre, *Buddenbrooks*. Regarding the servant status of her protagonist, Marie Ebner's novel could also be called a very early forerunner of Franz Werfel's *Barbara oder die Frömmigkeit* (Barbara or Piety) or Joseph Roth's *Napoleon oder die hundert Tage* (Napoleon or the Hundred Days), novels written in the 1920s and 30s respectively. In all three works servant women play a leading role. Like Roth's novel, dealing with the historic period of Napoleon's ultimate, but failing effort to regain power, Marie Ebner's *Božena* draws on historic facts "and makes them the pivot about which the fictional elements revolve."[3] Her novel's historic background is the Revolution of 1848, which brings death, destruction, and social change in its wake.

However, the plot focuses mainly on a Moravian maidservant, who has dedicated her life to serve her master's family. In the pursuit of this task she is willing to give up all personal happiness. Strong, courageous, and beautiful in both body and mind, she overcomes an early temptation to fall hopelessly in love with a handsome, but unfaithful and philandering man. Although her master, the wine merchant Heissenstein, is a tyrannical husband and father, she remains faithful to him and to his daughter Rosa and granddaughter, Röschen, for whom she acts as a shield. Through courage and perseverance and by overcoming seemingly impossible odds, Božena, in fact is ultimately able to ensure Röschen's happiness. Thus the young woman is enabled to obtain a full share of her rightful inheritance, previously denied her. On Božena's prodding, her mother's half-sister Regula agrees to give Röschen the house previously acquired from an impoverished aristocratic family. In this way, past efforts by Regula's mother, Heissenstein's second wife Nannete, to deprive Rosa and her daughter Röschen of their just dues are rectified. Röschen will find happiness there by the side of the previous owner's son.

As this subplot, tied into the novel's happy ending, makes clear, Marie Ebner is interested in exposing the timely theme of the sinking fortunes of some members of Austria's nobility after the Revolution of 1848. Not just in her narrative, but also in real life they were pushed out of their inherited estates by the upwardly mobile and newly monied bourgeoisie. As in other narratives of hers, childlessness—or, as we have it here, in a slight variant of her perennial concern, not having the "right" child—is also an important theme in this novel. It is introduced in the expository part of the work, in which Heissenstein mourns over the loss of a son: "It took a long time for Heissenstein to learn that his loss was real. . . 'For whom was I working?—I have no heir'" (Hafis, 3:10). He therefore does not find it too difficult to reject Rosa, his strong-willed daughter by his first wife. Not only is she unable to replace the deceased son in his heart. But unlike her gentle and compliant mother, Rosa is also a fighter: "Her mother would have lowered her head, she lifted it up—her mother would have avoided a fight, she joined right in . . ." (50).

This female assertiveness on the part of his daughter goes very much against Heissenstein's grain. To make matters worse, Rosa ignores her father's objections completely and marries Lieutenant von Fehse, whom she dearly loves. As a consequence, she is forced to leave her father's home, never to set foot in it again. Božena follows her and takes care of her and of her daughter Röschen, who after the unexpected early death of both parents is left an orphan. After experiencing and warding off much hardship, the servant woman, at the end of the novel, looks forward to nursing a third generation of Heissenstein offspring. Her old master and his daughter Rosa have passed on, but Röschen, owner now of the Rondsperg estate and happily married to young Ronald Rondsperg, will ensure the continuation of both families.

Reflecting on Marie Ebner's own experience with her father and her early marriage to a military officer, one can readily see that she crafted her novel figure Rosa very much in her own image, projecting in Röschen the daughter she innately longed to have but was denied by fate and physical circumstances. Yet Kurt Binneberg, editor and commentator of a recent historical and critical edition of the novel, calls the struggle for wealth the most important motif influencing the action of the novel. According to him, it penetrates the bourgeois circle of the wine merchant and the aristocratic realm of the Rondspergs.[4] But his argument of wealth's omnipotent role in this tale appears one-sided. In addition to the personal considerations stated above, Marie Ebner assigned an important function to rearing and education in the story. Yet, here too, the author lets the reader know that neither is a magic wand, as Regula's character and behavior prove.

Even the best training and conditioning cannot overcome inherent character flaws. Much more important than *Bildung* (education) as such is *Herzensbildung* (development of feelings), which is shown to involve altruistic feelings, compassion, empathy, and love. Regula has nothing to offer along these lines. Like her mother, she is a conniver given to intrigue. Her whole personality reflects her calculating, self-serving mind. Devoid of empathy and compassion, she is nonetheless a passionate person. But her passions are self-centered. Her most burning desire is to enhance her social standing in such a way that it reflects her material well-being. She longs to be part of the aristocracy. The very fact that she fails in this pursuit leads to an acute case of frustration and gives the outcome of the novel almost comic quaity. Instead of getting the handsome aristocrat, for whom she yearns, she must settle for a comic and scatterbrained commoner, who is at best a pseudointellectual. Božena is the exact opposite of Regula. She has little education in a formal setting but is by nature caring, compassionate, loving, and utterly selfless. Having no child of her own, she is both a mother and a servant to her ward Rosa and to the latter's daughter Röschen. The story's happy ending nonetheless provokes second thoughts about the master-servant relationship as practiced and socially condoned, indeed even lauded, in those days.

The genesis of the novel can be traced back to Marie Ebner's correspondence in 1875 with her brother Victor and her publisher Rodenberg, whose name may have inspired her to call the sympathetic aristocratic family in her novel Rondsperg. Quite influential were also Ida Fleischl's suggestions, which can be gleaned from diary entries by the authoress. The reception of the work on the part of the contemporary reading public, even though largely favorable, signifies little about its quality. It is of interest though because it reflects on the taste of the reading public of Marie Ebner's days. Much more important, however, seem Ferdinand von Saar's remarks to her in a personal letter: "Your *Božena* was most refreshing and pure pleasure. . . . The story is an excellent piece of writing."[5]

The reviews of the work's first edition of 1876 are also largely positive, although quite limited in number, written overwhelmingly by writers—Betty Paoli, Hieronymus Lorm, and Adam Wolf—with whom Marie Ebner was well acquainted. Yet these favorable signs notwithstanding, her book did not sell well. This very fact as well as her habit of seeking to achieve perfection led her to revise the novel in 1895. Other stylistically improved editions appeared during her lifetime, totaling eleven. Five more were published posthumously by Cotta. *Božena* was also translated during her lifetime into Czech and French.

Early literary criticism dwelt on the ethics and the tragic core of the novel. Erich Schmidt, a leading literary critic of the epoch, spoke of its "moral fundament of granite" (228). He refers here to Božena's unerring steadfastness of character nurtured by her devotion to Heissenstein and his daughter and granddaughter. Maria Franziska Radke, a later critic, focused on the duality of the heroine's tragic guilt in her study *Das Tragische in den Erzählungen von Marie von Ebner-Eschenbach* (The Tragic Element in the Stories of Marie von Ebner-Eschenbach), a focus also pursued by Heinz Rieder in his dissertation, "Die Gemeinschaft in den Erzählungen der Marie von Ebner-Eschenbach" (The Community in the Stories of Marie von Ebner-Eschenbach) (228-229). Both studies point out that in order to be a faithful servant, Božena must sacrifice all claims to any personal happiness of her own. But in so doing she becomes unfaithful to herself, denying in essence any craving of the heart. But what other choice does she have? When she succumbed temporarily in younger years to the wooing of an insincere gallant, she was doubly punished. Not only did she have to suffer the pain of ultimate rejection by the philandering man, but she also became painfully aware of her own shortcomings in her devotion to her master. The modern reader may have difficulty in appreciating Božena's psychological dilemma. But the practice of service has its historical roots in the German moral code of the middle ages, with which the German reading public of the nineteenth century was still well acquainted. Moreover, by accepting the role that fate seemed to have destined for her, she played into the hands of another well received contemporary notion: *Resignation.*

The sociocritical and socioethical aspects of the story, dealing with the social conditions that it exposes, were stressed by such analysts as Heideline Fink, Oskar Walzel, and in the dissertation of Ingeborg Geserick. The latter also dealt with the element of pedagogy in *Božena,* while Walzel approached it from the Romantic perspective. All of these interpretations point to the richness of the novel's plot (230-231). The novel's heroine is one of the most significant female characters in Marie Ebner's narrative opus. Clearly the author empathizes with her heroine and, especially in Božena's symbolic role of serving others, occasionally even identifies with her. If one considers Ebner's own upbringing, one can easily discern a distinct autobiographical bias in her story line. Her childhood nanny Pepinka was undoubtedly her primary source of inspiration in the crafting of her female protagonist. As in many of her earlier and later narratives, the strained relation between a father figure and his daughter, leading to a near Cinderella status of the latter, also has its origin in the author's own youthful experiences.

Literary analysis has also pointed to the duality of locale in the novel, centered in Weinberg and Rondsperg. "Both locales show distinct qualitative differences in tandem with the social standing of their respective inhabitants. This is reflected in the spatial narrowness of the one place and the wide openness of the other. . . . In spite of these differences, both locales are entwined with one another thorough the manifold interests of their respective inhabitants" (249-250). To be sure, both place-names, Weinberg and Rondsperg, seem to have emblematic meanings as well. The first alludes to Heissenstein's being a wine merchant. The latter reflects— aside from the possible personal connotation already mentioned—the positive climax of the story, the plot of which has come full circle to a happy ending for the offspring of both families through Röschen's and Ronald's union. This ultimate harmony, extending also to the social climate of the story, is underlined by the alliterative nature of their first names.

The time structure, as Binneberg has pointed out, is vague at the beginning. We do not find any time reference prior to the ninth chapter, when the text cites the summer of 1847. Then the plot is intertwined with the revolutionary happenings of 1848. On closer scrutiny the Weinberg action extends to roughly thirty years. Time also plays a role in the Rondsperg segment. Like the wine merchant, the estate owner is hopeful that his place can be passed on to future generations.

The numerous biblical, literary, and popular quotations in the novel capture the reader's attention. Religious citations are principally encountered in the family setting of the wine merchant Heissenstein (28O). While the interspersed popular sayings have cliché character, the quotations taken from literary sources reveal the acquaintances of the author with French and German classics. Viewed in a critical sense, however, Marie Ebner's first novel betrays in many of its segments a lack of central focus. This fact was not lost on Louise von François, who criticized the work from this aspect in an early letter:

> You are not faithful enough to your heroine, the noble
> and strong-willed servant woman, pushing her aside
> barely after we begin to warm up to her, and putting
> minor characters in the foreground, who cannot cap-
> ture our interest in the same way. . . . If you would
> have given the life history of this servant woman with-
> out interruption, . . . we would have such a touching
> novel that only few others would measure up to it.
> For Božena is a character of Shakespearean originality
> and depth. (263)

While *Božena* can in spite of certain weaknesses be
looked upon as a modern literary monument to the faithfulness of a servant toward a master, bringing to mind earlier
and prototypical literary examples of such dedication and fidelity as, for example, those incorporated in the *Nibelungen-
lied* (Lay of the Nibelungs)—which reflected the ethos of
past generations—Marie Ebner's second novel, *Das Gemeindekind* (The Ward of the Parish, 1887), is more forward-looking. It is also more centrally focused. This narrative, which
can be designated as both a *Bildungsroman* and an *Entwicklingsroman,* is a supreme reflection of Maria Ebner's belief
in the individual's capacity for growth, no matter how
formidable the obstacles. It is also an acknowledgment on the
part of the author that in her view the inner forces of a given
human nature, if properly stimulated and applied, are stronger
than an unfavorable environment or unsavory social milieu.

Such beliefs, however, fly in the face of modern sociological theory, which places nurture over nature or, if one
will, environmental over hereditary factors in its attempt to
predict or interpret human behavior and development, but

still considers both to be crucial determinants of human character. Yet in Marie Ebner's novel both the heredity and environment of the main character are gravely flawed.. Her protagonist Pavel Holut, in effect, is the antithesis of modern hereditary and milieu theories, expounded and adopted by the writers of literary Naturalism, which was at its greatest peak of popularity when Ebner wrote her novel. Thus the generally despised and consequently wild and recalcitrant Pavel, son of a convicted murderer who had been executed for robbing and killing a priest, does not follow in his father's footsteps. Despite the fact that his mother has also been convicted as an accomplice in the crime and sent to jail for ten years, he eventually overcomes the negative effects of his milieu and background to become a decent, fully functioning and contributing member of society.

To be sure, his mother, as is soon revealed, was not an inherently evil woman in spite of her conviction. She was, in fact, a victim of wife abuse. During her husband's trial she refused to testify against him out of fear of retribution. But it was her very silence that implicated her in the crime: "They shouted to her in vain: 'You are signing your own death warrant!'"—it left no impression on her, nor did it frighten her. She was not afraid of the judges, nor of death. She feared 'her husband'" (Hafis, 1:12).

While Pavel after his parents' conviction becomes the ward of a small Moravian village community that does not really want to take care of him properly and therefore has the village swine herdsman raise him in a substandard social setting, his sister Milanda is blessed in finding a kind noblewoman to look after her. Pavel's foster-father, on the other hand, is a drunkard and a member of the village underclass. Pavel's early training in school and at the squalid place he is forced to call his home consists consequently mainly of scorn. As a result he begins to hate everybody, withdrawing almost totally within himself. He reaches his life's nadir when he is wrongly and maliciously accused of having poisoned the village mayor. But after having been prompted by his sister, whom he loves dearly, to change his ways and on being fortunate in finding a school teacher who takes the interest in helping him to learn and grow, Pavel undergoes a complete transformation. He becomes an entirely different person now, opening his heart and mind to the world around him and to other people. Eventually he even acquires a run-down property to have a home of his own. The narrator comments on this humble abode: "Poverty was looking through the three low windows. But he who knew how to read invisible inscriptions saw the print over the narrow door: Diligence enters through me, which will conquer this poverty" (131-132). Yet despite this remarkable turnaround in his life, he is not spared new tragedy. His beloved sister Milanda, who earlier decided to become a nun, succumbs to illness. Ultimately, though, he regains some measure of happiness and satisfaction on being able to take care of his mother after her release from prison.

The novel is replete with social commentary and authorial observations of both timely and timeless import, such as the schoolmaster's remarks, whose name Habrecht symbolizes Marie Ebner's social and pedagogical convictions:

> Pay attention! We live in an exceptionally instructive age. Never before have we been preached a clearer message: Be selfless, if for no other, nobler reason, at least for the sake of preservation of self. . . . In previous ages, one could sit before a full plate and dig in without worrying that the plate of his neighbor was empty. That is impossible now, unless one belongs to the intellectually blind. (189)

Quite personal and uncannily prophetic about the world-
wide population explosion of the second half of the twentieth
century is the following admonition: "Everyone does not
need to establish a family. It is the greatest illusion to believe
that everybody has to have his own children.— There are
enough children in the world" (190). Habrecht is also the one
who raises the specter of nationalistic strife in the Empire
and admonishes against it:

> When I heard that, the horrible apparition of which I
> spoke in the beginning grinned at me. . . . One more
> thing! They are much more belligerently Czech there
> than here. My German name bothered them. They
> looked for German nationalist sentiments in me, in
> me, for whom the whole earth is a dreadful place and
> everybody on it bears a more or less heavy burden!
> . . . There is one nation, indeed one, which guides,
> which shines as a beacon: all productive people,—I
> would be proud to be part of it. . . . As far as every
> other pride of nationality is concerned, . . . idiocy, un-
> worthy of this country. (185)

These words make it clear that Marie Ebner's innermost sympathies—which she has her mouthpiece Habrecht express—
transcend even those which she naturally felt toward the Austrian supranational monarchy. She alludes in this instance to
a strong bond with "all productive people." This is an unmistakable betrayal of her strong cosmopolitan beliefs.

Das Gemeindekind, her generally acknowledged masterpiece in novel form, is prefaced with the French saying:
"Tout est l'histoire." By that, however, the authoress did not
only mean the actions unleashed by the impersonal forces of
history, but also the deeds committed by the common folk.
This work reveals more clearly than any other she ever wrote

the vast potential for both the good and the bad in the lower classes. But rather than focusing on the weaknesses of the common people and the danger that they might pose to the status quo, the author concentrates on an exceptional individual in their midst and his nearly miraculous development toward higher grounds of social and political maturity. Thus the novel could rightfully be called the developmental novel of the lowly and unimportant. Doubtless, this approach to the subgenre of *Bildungsroman* is beholden to the age of positivism, Naturalism, and unfolding socialism, which came into its own in the 1880s with its discussions about nurture and nature, environment and heredity, and their respective influence on the shaping of human behavior in terms of its effect, if not its political consequences, in a modern mass society. It is also a clear indication that Ebner resolved to place the action of her narrative outside the artistic and narrowly individualistic confines of the traditional *Entwicklungsroman* and to put it squarely into the social arena.

Rainer Baasner revealed in his critical edition of the novel that Marie Ebner had written several versions. Yet none of the manuscripts of this work was preserved. Presumably completed by October 24, 1886, the final version was first published in the February to May 1887 issue of the *Rundschau* (Panorama). Its plot is based on actual events that were reported in a feuilleton of the *Wiener Freie Presse* (Vienna Free Press) on October 29, 1887, one year after the completion of the work. Marie Ebner approached her close friends Ida Fleischl and Rodenberg with the request of reading various completed chapters prior to publication. She asked them for advice on their merit. Rodenberg's reaction was highly complimentary:

> The story line, as far as I can judge it at this point, is beautifully developed; the composition lucid, clear, the

depiction of characters firm; the style above reproach
and the totality of it is glazed with a film of nobility
and gentleness—if . . . the rest and the end correspond
to the excerpts before me, you have created a masterpiece which will endure in German literature and
which, if brought out first by the *Rundschau,* will considerably enhance its reputation.[6]

However, as was the case with her first novel, *Das Gemeindekind* also elicited but little interest immediately after
publication. The first comprehensive review was undertaken
by her later interpreter and biographer Anton Bettelheim. He
praised the pedagogical intent of the work, the profound
humanity of the author, and her narrative skills (197). Yet he
and other early reviewers of the novel were also critical of
the overly positive and optimistic ending of the story. They
were influenced by the then prevalent theories of Naturalism.
The probability that the impoverished and abandoned son of
a murderer, who had become the despised and rejected ward
of a rural parish, could ultimately grow into a solid and contributing member of society seemed very remote to them.
They had difficulty in believing that there could be potential
good in what, by all appearances, was nothing but evil. Still,
the majority of subsequent reviews were favorable. Two of
the most influential were published in *Westermanns Illustri-
erte Monatshefte* (Westermann's Illustrated Monthly) and in
Franzos's *Deutsche Dichtung* (German Literature). The well-
known critic Erich Schmidt reviewed the novel in an equally
complimentary way. As a consequence readers became more
interested in the work and it could go through nine editions.
In the 1890s a special dispensation was given by the publisher Paetel, allowing publication of the narrative in serial form
in the *Wiener Arbeiterzeitung* (Vienna Workers Daily). The
novel's appearance in this popular daily helped to spread its

appeal among the general reading public even more. As the fame of the work grew and spread, translations of it were also undertaken in Holland and in the United States. Parallel to Marie Ebner's growing international reputation, the narrative became ever more popular at home as well. Paul Wiegler was among the first to call *Das Gemeindekind* a social novel and to rank it as "the most important realistic prose of the authoress" (227).[7] Some critics attempted to connect the work with the Naturalist theories of nurture versus nature and heredity versus environment. Baasner does not share this view and would not include Ebner-Eschenbach among Naturalist writers. He nevertheless concedes that her language and style are somewhat influenced by the currents of literary Naturalism: "The vocabulary that Marie von Ebner-Eschenbach employs is to a great extent that of an elevated everyday language. This feature increases its clarity and its realistic appearance" (332). As can be seen, Marie Ebner is not easy to label or to categorize. In the same way in which she was able to develop her writing skills in all the major genres of literary endeavor except poetry, she also tended to absorb and to amalgamate the literary currents of her epoch without, however, clearly favoring the one or the other consistently. It might do well to call her an eclectic. Be this as it may, the work's reputation and popularity have remained high and undiminished to the present day. The primary reason for this lies in its timeless and touching social message which has successfully transcended philological and narrowly defined stylistic considerations.

Marie Ebner's third novel, *Unsühnbar* (Inexpiable), which was first published in serial form in *Deutsche Rundschau* in 1889, leaves the broad social sphere and turns from general societal concerns, as expressed in *Das Gemeindekind,* to focus on high society. It deals, in effect, with the goings-on in the august and normally closed circles of Austrian aristocracy toward the end of the nineteenth century. But rather than presenting an exposé of this class, the author, an insider herself, relates the story of a noblewoman, who in the course of her marriage breaks her vows of fidelity to her husband. The outcome is tragic. She ultimately destroys herself because of her pronounced feelings that she has committed a moral crime that is unforgivable and inexpiable. One can easily trace earlier versions of this central motif of female culpability to Marie Ebner's dramatic beginnings, where it is especially pronounced in *Maria Stuart in Schottland* and in *Marie Roland*. The fact that she also names her doomed heroine in *Unsühnbar* Maria is—as was the case in her dramas—indicative of her very close and personal attachment to this generic character in her oeuvre. The motif of female culpability also plays an important function in *Božena,* except for the fact that in this, her first novel, the heroine is able to overcome the temptation of the flesh and to pursue her basic and prescribed role of service unimpeded. Not so in *Unsühnbar.* The passion of the moment overpowers the moral core, the conscience, of the novel's central figure in such a way that she commits a morally and socially unforgivable act: engaging in extramarital sex. After much soul-searching she sees no other means of expiating her guilt but to destroy her reputation and to forfeit her life.

The focus of the plot on a fatal weakness in the protagonist and the tragic consequences issuing therefrom brings to mind two earlier novels that made history in nineteenth-century European letters: Flaubert's *Madame Bovary* and Tolstoy's *Anna Karenina.* Considering Marie Ebner's extraordinary and well-documented love of reading and her extensive knowledge of past and present European literature, it can be assumed that she was familiar with these two influential books. Aside from the fact that Ebner is the first female author of renown in Austro-German letters to deal with this popular theme, it is worth noting that her novel predates Theodor Fontane's *Effi Briest,* the most famous rendering of adultery and its fatal consequences in a woman's life in German letters. Previously, Louise von François, with whom Marie Ebner corresponded for years and who had long been a role model for her, called *Unsühnbar* "an Austrian *Anna Karenina.*"[8] But it should not be overlooked that Ebner took some of the details of her novel from a widely discussed occurrence that had actually taken place in contemporary Austrian aristocratic circles.

The novel concerns the proud and beautiful Countess Maria Wolfsberg, who cannot forgive her father for having driven her mother into madness and early death because of his illicit love affair with another woman. Convinced of her own moral fortitude and strength, she marries Dornach, a man of her social standing, although she is not really in love with him. She subsequently falls victim to the guiles of the demonic womanizer Tessin and bears him a son. She does not find the courage to inform her husband of her trespass, and he considers the child to be his own. Her fear of being exposed to shame and derision becomes all-consuming, but is basically groundless, for no one, least of all her husband, suspects her of any wrongdoing. Only her father seems to sense the truth. After her husband and the couple's older boy, who is legitimately his, die in a boating accident, Maria feels compelled to go public with her story of marital infidelity. So severe are her feelings of guilt that she reveals all, in so doing, however, she not only destroys her own reputation, but also ruins the standing and status of her remaining, totally innocent child, a bastard as it were, conceived out of wedlock. True, Maria was able to obtain forgiveness from a priest, whom she had sought out, but she still cannot forgive herself. Even after seeking to find her own path to God, she is unable to overcome her strong feelings of guilt. The following thoughts crossing her mind betray her moral agony in this endeavor: "Your doing, You incomprehensible, unknown God. . . . She recalled a saying which she read in an old book . . . : 'His providential role you may hate, / But the artist in Him you cannot berate.'" (Hafis, 2:291).

This central focus notwithstanding, the author also takes occasion to criticize her own social class, the high society of Austrian nobility, as she had done in some of her previous works. In this instance she casts a critical eye at the various wasteful and socially useless indulgences some of her peers engage in, extending from addiction to expensive Turkish tobaccos to the death hunt of forest animals and even spiritualism, which, one lady predicts, would become the official state religion one day.[9] In-fighting for social prestige is also a very popular pastime among these privileged people: "A sort of armed peace prevailed there. It was open, mutual enmity; rooted dishonesty and deceitfulness on the part of the weak, stubbornness and unremitting harshness on the part of the strong" (195).

Burkhard Bittrich reveals in his historico-critical edition of *Unsühnbar* that Marie Ebner began writing the manuscript of the novel on May 8, 1888, and sent the last two chapters of the work to Rodenberg on July 1, 1889. They were printed the same year in the December edition of *Deutsche Rundschau*. The original manuscript, however, appears to be irretrievably lost. The novel's first book edition came out in March 1890. The essential difference between the book text and the magazine version is minuscule. It consists essentially in the elimination of five foreign words in the text and the substitution of them by German equivalents. Otherwise, only a few minor stylistic changes were undertaken.[10]

The first known critical review of the novel appeared in the *Allgemeine Zeitung* (General Daily) of April 10, 1890, in which a nameless critic attacked the psychological viability and the overall believability of the heroine's character:

> The blow [of Maria's sinfulness] strikes the reader
> quite unexpectedly, without warning; the reprehensible
> deed enters the story like a *deus ex machina.* A deep
> split appears in Maria's character and no reader will
> be able to bridge it using the information provided by
> the authoress" (250).

The literary critic Moritz Necker, an early admirer of Marie
Necker, rejected this criticism in his article "Marie Ebner und
der Wiener Adel" (Marie Ebner and Vienna's Aristocracy),
printed in the May 1890 edition of the *Grenzbote* (Border
Courier). Yet the controversy continued. Fritz Mauthner, another literary critic, voiced his misgivings. Bruno Walden
gave a mixed review in the *Wiener Zeitung* (Vienna Daily)
of April 25, 1890.[11] Distinctly more favorable was the
commentary of Paul Szczenpański in *Velhagen und Klasings
Neue Monatshefte* (Velhagen's and Klasing's New Monthly)
(254). The well-known academic critic, Erich Schmidt, on the
other hand, questioned the uniformity in the makeup of
Maria's character. The much respected and widely read Austrian writer and critic Peter Rosegger considered all of the
novel's characters to be too idealized in his review of July
1890, appearing in the literary magazine *Heimgarten* (Home
Journal) (258). These criticisms caused Marie Ebner to under-
take three extensive revisions. A fourth was to follow. The
novel appeared in nine editions extending to 1911. It was
finally incorporated in Ebner-Eschenbach's *Gesammelte
Schriften* (Collected Works, 1920) after her death.

Twenty years earlier, the Grillparzer specialist August
Sauer found words of praise for *Unsühnbar* in a lecture given
in Vienna on October 30, 1900. When Ebner's fame began
to diminish later in the twentieth century, the soundness of

the psychological basis of the heroine's character depiction was questioned again by such literary historians as Rudolf Latzke, who earlier had given a cautious evaluation of *Unsühnbar* in his *Deutsch-österreichische Literaturgeschichte* (Austro-German Literary History), and by Werner Kohlschmidt in his more recent critique in volume four of his *Geschichte der deutschen Literatur von den Anfängen bis zur Gegenwart* (History of German Literature from the Beginning to the Present). Burkhard Bittrich comments:

> The preponderantly negative verdict of more recent research concerning *Unsühnbar* is also reflected in the fact that this work of Ebner . . . is almost completely left out in novel guides and literary encyclopedias. Compared with the favored larger tales, *Das Gemeindekind* and *Božena*, it is banished, so to speak, together with the really poor *Die arme Kleine* to last place. Erich Schmidt's condemnation is still effective. (295)

The reputation of the work and its critical reception are, it seems, inextricably intertwined with the character of Maria Wolfsberg-Dornach. The question still debated by the work's critics is essentially this: Are the transgression and expiation of the young countess believable? The question seems to be academic and unwarranted, however, inasmuch as this crucial core of the story is based on an actual occurrence rather than being a figment of Ebner's artistic imagination. One should also not fault her for not having provided enough background leading up to her heroine's disgrace. Outwardly, Wolfsberg and Tessin occupy opposite positions in the plot, but they are essentially two chips off the same block. They are not only passionate womanizers, but also collaborators in the heroine's downfall, even though Wolfsberg's part in this is coincidental. Yet the tragic ending of the novel still goes one step further. It is the direct and logical result of a novella-like happening, a Goethean "unprecedented past event": a highly respected woman of the highest stratum of Austrian nobility accuses herself of adultery in public and exposes her only remaining child as being illegitimate.

The structure of the story seems also well balanced. Bittrich comes to the same conclusion regarding the novel's time element by stating that "Erzählzeit und erzählte Zeit" (the time in which a story is told and the time a story covers) roughly correspond with one another (319). Stylistic leitmotifs appear and reappear in such words as *gut* (good), *Güte* (kindness), *sühnen* (to expiate), and *unsühnbar* (inexpiable), the latter in direct reference to the novel's title (332). Bittrich sees *Unsühnbar* as fitting in well with the tradition of the nineteenth-century *Eheroman* (novel of marriage). He calls the work also a philosophical novel, dealing with the modern notions of truth and free will. Just as modern is Marie Ebner's view of the remoteness of God (339-341).

An additional theme deserving recognition is that of derangement and possible mental illness in women. Both Maria and previously her mother suffer psychic breakdowns of such severity that the results are catastrophic and fatal. Marie Ebner, who experienced lower levels of psychic dysfunction in her own life, also treated this theme in her shorter narratives *Margarete* and *Das Schädliche*. The heroine's impulsive action in *Unsühnbar* of needlessly revealing her totally unsuspected marital infidelity in an attempt of public expiation appears to be both futile and deranged. It defies rational explanations, as reviewers had pointed out. It is also an unwarranted act from a moral and even religious point of view, since it irretrievably ruins the reputation of her surviving and completely innocent son. It can only be ascribed to an emotional decision by a woman whose psychic equilibrium has been severely damaged. Previous critical analysis notwithstanding, this interpretation would go a long way toward rehabilitating the novel's unjustly tarnished reputation.

Marie Ebner's fourth larger narrative is *Glaubenslos?* (Without Faith?, 1893). It continues to unveil her interest in popular and traditional views about God, faith, and religion. What makes this—to use her own words—*Erzählung* into a novel, however, are not just its metaphysical and philosophical concerns, but their societal and sociological ramifications. Like *Das Gemeindekind*, the novel *Glaubenslos?* also contains all the basic elements of an *Entwicklingsroman*. The very question mark at the end of the title provides an initial clue regarding the development of the work's central character in the area of most concern to him: faith in God.

The novel's plot deals essentially with the torment within the psyche of a young country priest. After discovering the world's imperfections and man's shortcomings, Father Leo Klinger is so shaken in his religious idealism and faith that he is contemplating leaving the priesthood he had entered full of youthful idealism and with the highest expectations. But on encountering the base nature of the simple country folk he is to serve and on fathoming the inherent evil in their character, their hypocrisy, and their superficial and feigned piousness, his own faith in God and His design is faltering. He divulges his doubts in God and in his own mission to his superior, Parson Thalberg, the village priest. The kind old priest advises him not to reason with his faith, but to follow the precepts and commandments of the church, although, as it turns out, he has not always adhered to these principles himself, a lapse which has led to reprimands by the office of the bishop. It becomes obvious that Thalberg, who has gained experience in the ways of man and the world—as his symbolic name also confirms, reflecting his priestly functions in the valleys and on mountains—treats Pater Leo like the son he never had. Yet the young priest bemoans not only the moral want of the local populace he has been told to serve, but also his own inability to change these people. The very sense of his mission, nurtured by his faith in God is at stake: "Reverend! And with these killers of souls we waste our lives away; and the best in us is used up on their incorrigibility!" (Hafis, 2:50). He is ready to quit his calling, but the old priest musters his considerable persuasive power to convince him otherwise.

> "You fool, you fool! . . . What are the scrimmages you want to avoid compared with the storm awaiting you on the outside!" He wants to go out into the world, in which the hatred of all against all rages and storms—in which everybody is unforgiving; in which the person on your side may do his worst unscathed and your opponent may not do his best unscathed; in which one nation takes up arms against another, as does one class against another and even one sex against the other. And what weapons, oh God, Lord! Not those of an honest war, in which the soldier respects in his enemy his fellow human being and in this way himself—but a war with despicable weapons, for the arrows which swirl about and hit their targets are dipped in the venom of slander. . . . We see how science is abused in the service of murder. We see our godly religion of love, of the highest tolerance, of the most profound humility, desecrated into a tool of ambition, of lust for power. . . . "What do you expect to achieve—you—with your peaceful heart, in this world of hatred?" (54-55)

Truly, more powerful, but also more truthful and prophetic words indicting mankind for lacking humanity could not have been spoken by anyone of Marie Ebner's generation. How prescient that Thalberg exclaims them nearly twenty years before the onset of the cataclysmic First World War, the biggest and most deadly bloodletting yet known to man. It should also not be overlooked that these views reflected both her father's and her husband's beliefs. Doubtless, the latter, a military scientist, revealed his innermost fears to her about the inevitability of such a cataclysmic conflict. Yet the years prior to that war were generally a time of supreme optimism in the supposedly unceasing onward and upward movement of civilization and human enlightenment.

Initially, Pater Leo does not heed these words of wisdom and insight by his mentor. He remains doubtful and unconvinced about his calling. He is a naive, but rebellious seeker of truth like Franzos's Georg Winter,[12] a novel hero of contemporary vintage, or Hermann Hesse's Siddharta, whose quests were to be related a generation later. Just like these two protagonists, Pater Leo cannot learn vicariously; he cannot find the truth in the experiences or observations and insight of others, no matter how convincingly they may be related to him. A change of heart or direction and salvation for him in the Christian sense can only come from the rekindling of his own faith in God and His design. By extension, then, Pater Leo must find a way back to his original sense of mission. He must regenerate his desire to serve the people who have been entrusted to his care and to guide them lovingly again onto the path of righteousness and love of their fellow man.

This motif gives the novel autobiographical connotations. Although raised a Catholic, Marie Ebner left this tradition gradually in an intellectual as well as in a spiritual sense in order to find a new and personal faith of her own in a sort of moral theism. With the passing of time and the gaining of new insights, she was able to develop this personal faith further in the direction of moral rectitude. In *Glaubenslos?*, the young priest's dilemma is resolved along these lines as well. Thus when put to the supreme test, he finds the strength and the wisdom to help the true non-believer, the invalid peasant-farmer Kogler, who had terrorized his family, to die in peace. The priest also guides Kogler's farmhand Sepp, who almost murdered Kogler because of the wrong he did to his daughter Vroni, back to his own better self. Only after Kogler's widow thanks Pater Leo for helping them over their difficulties does he realize his power to do good. He asks the astonished woman to give her consent to a union between Sepp and Vroni. Although Sepp is but a farmhand without worldly possessions, she agrees to the marriage. Encouraged by the widow's positive reply and her admiration for him, Pater Leo will stay and continue to serve as a priest, as a healer of souls, and as a bridge builder between man and God.

The positive and optimistic ending of this novel with its emphasis on service to mankind gives the work a truly Goethean imprimatur and makes the *Entwicklungsroman* a true *Bildungsroman*. The same cannot be said at all with regard to Marie Ebner's last major narrative, the short novel *Agave* (1903). To be sure, its main character, the Renaissance painter Antonio Venesco, undergoes a development. But his developmental path in this *Künstlerroman* (artist novel)—a popular subgenre in German literature—leads him in the opposite direction. The sudden loss of artistic genius in a young person, which Marie Ebner witnessed around the time this novel was written in her young contemporary and fellow Austrian Hugo von Hofmannsthal (1874-1929), is indeed a tragic event. This brilliant poet, essayist, dramatist, librettist, and writer of prose works experienced a sudden and— unknown to him and others at the time—temporary loss of poetic focus around the turn of the century. Celebrated as the literary *Wunderkind* in German letters of the 1890s, his poetic genius appeared to have reached the critical stage of burnout when he published his *Ein Brief: Brief des Lord Chandos* (A Letter: Letter of Lord Chandos, 1902). In the letter, addressed to his alleged friend, the sixteenth and early seventeenth century philosopher, statesman, and scientist Francis Bacon, the fictitious writer looks back at his rich poetic production of previous years. He excuses himself for suddenly falling silent, ascribing this silence to the spiritual and intellectual dilemma of a writer who suddenly despairs of language, yet is incapable of interpreting, or even understanding, the cause.

The symbolic name which Ebner gave to her narrative, dealing with this phenomenon in the art field, establishes a relationship between the rare and miraculous plant of the title, which blooms only once, and the youthful Antonio, student of the great Renaissance painter Masaccio. Under the spell of both love and pain, he creates only one masterful painting and loses his genius thereafter. In spite of numerous tries, he is unable to recapture the indefinable artistic inspiration and skill to equal his initial masterpiece. What is worse, no matter how much he tries, he does not even come close. In this story, the author, under the personal spell of her earlier visit to Italy, also left the territory of the old Austrian monarchy, the locale of her other tales, to venture south of the border and, timewise, into a rather distant historic past. This is the only time that she ever attempted to do both in a larger narrative work. Despite her painstaking historical research and the ample historical details she provided in her characters and in the story background, the work has been criticized, as Lackner pointed out, for lacking her usual personal touch.[13] But, as her biography makes clear, Marie Ebner shared significant experience with the novel's main character. She knew the pain of failure as an artist. Although her own development as a writer did not equal or parallel that of her novel hero, she had experienced the loss of confidence and the depth of despair to which he is subjected.

The direction which the development of the novel's protagonist will take is symbolically foretold in the verses preceding the work:

> Made of transparency, Agave, art thou,
> Created in beauty, rare art thou
> Like flowers in a fairy tale, awakened through magic.
> On a dainty stalk, wreathed around it, thou riseth,
> Scarcely created, yet perfectly done.
> For an intoxicating spring, Agave,
> Thou giveth away the endurance of a lifetime
> And vanisheth in bloom—thou art a miracle.

The story unfolds during Italy's golden age. Antonio leaves
home and plans to perfect his skills as a painter and to seek
fame and fortune. He achieves the former only temporarily.
Prior to reaching this goal, however, he must experience bitter disappointment. His lover and betrothed, the beautiful
Margherita, leaves him for a wealthy man. Longing for the
good life, she did not want to share his ardor for art and the
hardships associated with pursuing it. Antonio, who dearly
loves her, is in a state of total devastation. He vanishes from
public sight and appears months later, on the verge of mental
and physical exhaustion. Yet, miraculously, he has created a
most unusual tripartite painting, depicting Margherita as personification of love, passion, and hatred. The experts judge
it to be a masterpiece. The duke of Florence, on hearing of
Antonio's newly gained fame, invites him to his court. Yet
Antonio's happiness there as an artist and painter in residence
is of short duration. Even though he is told to create more
masterful paintings, he is incapable of doing so. Whatever
genius he had, it has left him. In spite of several attempts, he
cannot paint anything of value.

Only one person understands his agony and sympathizes with his pain. It is the beautiful, widowed daughter of the duke, Judith Altovita. Soon they become secret lovers. After Antonio realizes, however, that he will never be able to equal his first and only masterpiece, he destroys all of his other paintings in a fit of madness. On being told to leave the court, Judith expresses her willingness to share his fate as his wife, provided that he pledge her his eternal love. Unable to do so, he leaves without her and without means. He wants to seek out Maestro Masaccio, hoping to recapture his erstwhile talent under the great man's guidance. But it is too late for that. The master dies before Antonio is able to see him. The story comes full circle. Antonio returns home to his old father to work again in the small family shop. Surprisingly, Margherita has shared a similar fate. She too becomes poor again after leaving her wealthy lover. Fulfilling a last request of Masaccio's gravely ill woman friend, Pulcheria Pisano, she visits Antonio in order to bring him comfort in his ordeal. After he overcomes his initial rage and his pent-up hatred for Margherita, the two former lovers finally find peace. They may start a modest life together.

This story, which was not as well received and is consequently not as well known as her other novels, is related in a fluid and captivating style. It is one of Marie Ebner's most passionate and erotic tales, capturing at the same time the patina of Renaissance Italy and the lives of artists of this milieu in a breathtaking and even thrilling manner. It is hard to believe that an old woman of seventy-three wrote it with so much passion and compassion. The characters, even though partly historical, are also well crafted and convincing in their roles. Antonio's male counterpart in the novel, his teacher Masaccio, loves art as dearly as Antonio does, but he lacks the latter's ambition to achieve fame for its own sake. Masaccio is a purist and an idealist. He has pursued art all his life as his highest goal and not as a means to attain fame and fortune. As is obvious, the two men occupy opposite poles of the emotive and intellectual spectrum.

The same can be said of the two female figures in the story, Margherita and Judith. Both bear symbolic names. The former is a distant relative of Margarete and shares some of her characteristics. Judith has the royal bearings and the passion of her biblical namesake. Yet both have distinct features of their own. Margherita is, at least initially, immature, uneven, and given to emotional gyrations that are less severe than those of Margarete, though she also follows her impulses of the moment. Judith is a passionate but mature woman and lover, willing to sacrifice her security and social standing for the sake of her beloved, but not of her people or her country. She gives more than she receives. Yet similar to her biblical model, her feelings are also genuine and come from the heart. Her demeanor, though, betrays a high level of intellectuality, which also puts her on opposite ends to Margherita. Ultimately it becomes evident that Marie Ebner reflects her own personality makeup, as it evolved over the years, in these fictional characters as well. Seen from this perspective, the old and experienced authoress is the composite figure of all of them. Thus she has the princess in a tête-à-tête with Antonio glorify love as "the crown of this life . . . its highest good . . ." (Hafis, 8:251) and, conversely, condemns the art work that portrays opposite sentiments and themes. Maestro Masaccio utters these words of indictment on rejecting the third and negative panel of Antonio's universally praised masterpiece: "This work of hatred! . . . Of hatred, which once was love; its child and its opposite. It shows the sacred light of beauty in this woman wiped out to its very last gleam. . . . No longer beautiful! . . . You terrible man! You murdered beauty, love!" (223). But Marie Ebner does not portray Margherita and Antonio, in spite of their evident shortcomings, in a truly negative fashion either. They reflect after all her own inner self in younger years, when she was equally immature and in search of recognition and fame.

Although *Agave* is, as we have seen, not her only story dealing with art and the artist, it is Marie Ebner's most intense and comprehensive treatment of this topic and also her most personal one. She experienced failure in the related artistic area of creative writing early in life herself and was able to overcome it and rise above it through diligence and a supreme effort of will power and positive thinking. It must be added though, that her elevated social status was of great advantage to her in this endeavor. The novel's protagonist is unable to do likewise, not least because of the latter. His are very modest socioeconomic roots. Hence he is ultimately forced to give up his quest and to return home as a total failure. The only one finding satisfaction in this is his father, who has never forgiven his son for neglecting his mother in her final hours of need:

> Thus nothing became of him! The dream of attaining the fame and fortune of an artist, it all dissipated . . . He had his longed-for revenge and could let his poor wife know in her grave that her son had not sinned against her unscathed. A feeling of triumph arose in him. Heavenly justice really existed. His curse had conjured it up. (273)

The evidence shows that all of Marie Ebner's novels, as is the case with most of her shorter stories, are narratives with built-in dramatic tension. The driving force within all of them is the psychic turmoil in their principal characters. Thus these narratives are not so much novels of ideas, although social criticism plays some role in them. They are also not stylistically or structurally complex. Their most outstanding

feature is the persistent focus on the development of the protagonists. In three of them—*Božena, Das Gemeindekind,* and
Glaubenslos?—the path which the main characters follow
leads them ultimately to positive ends and satisfactory goals.
In *Unsühnbar* and in *Agave,* however, no positive development of character can unfold. The psychological weaknesses
of the characters' inner makeup lead to fragile flaws. The
outcome, therefore, is not only negative, but also tragic. The
fact that three of her protagonists are male and two are
female seems to have little bearing on the direction their lives
take, although it should not be overlooked here that the
female figures are inherently restricted in their development
by social mores. Marie Ebner's own professional life as a
woman writer tends, in spite of the many ups and downs she
was bound to experience and some inevitable disappointments and sorrows, in the direction of her developmental
stories with positive endings. Since, because of her social
standing and lifelong financial security, she was never one of
those writers who had to strain and struggle to eke out a
living, writing was more of an avocation to her than a vocation. Yet, even if she did not look at writing as a means of
generating income, she was from the very beginning not beyond the urge to seek fame. After a protracted struggle, she
achieved at last a considerable amount of recognition as a
writer in her own lifetime. It remains to be investigated how
widespread it was and how long it lasted.

Chapter V

THE HUMANIST MESSAGE

Marie Ebner's story as a writer is not merely highlighted by many decades of creative activity and growth but also by steadfastness of purpose and commitment. Few writers have found the strength of character to continue with their calling in the face of so many obstacles. Her family was nearly united in strongly opposing her writing efforts. Many of her early literary critics were less than kind. What was even worse, however, was the fact that the public, whose support she craved, showed little initial interest in her works. Only her closest friends and advisers stood by her in her nearly manic determination to continue her efforts. But slowly and steadily the history of her reception began to turn in her favor. Growing numbers of critics and at last also the reading public began to appreciate her constantly expanding literary enterprise. A remarkable breakthrough, especially for a woman writer, had occurred.

Around the turn of the century and to her death in 1916, Marie von Ebner-Eschenbach was considered to be the *grande dame* of contemporary German letters. Slowly her fame had spread throughout the German-speaking world. She was much praised and widely read thanks to earlier efforts of admirers, friends, publishers and other writers such as Ida von Fleischl-Marxow, Louise von François, Karl Emil Franzos, Franz Grillparzer, Paul Heyse, Betty Paoli, Julius Rodenberg, Ferdinand von Saar, and Joseph von Weilen, to name some of the most prominent among them. But her favorable reception as an author also was, in no small measure, the result of the timeliness, readability, and overall attractiveness and excellence of her writings. At the same time, she was much admired and greatly honored as a person, especially in her native Austria. The public awaited, bought, and read the latest books of the indefatigable old lady, who appeared determined to continue to write as long as mind and body would permit her to do so. Both literary critics and the academic establishment gave her by and large a favorable press, guided by genuine admiration for her past and present literary achievements. Her contemporaries, in effect, paid homage to her literary skills and regarded her as the most gifted female writer of German letters and as a woman writer of international standing. August Sauer elaborates on this point:

> Of older German women writers, Annette v. Droste can be compared with her very well as to overall artistic merit and depth. In terms of versatility and breadth of vision, in artistic stature, she surpasses Louise v. François, whom she highly respected, and her passionate friend Betty Paoli. She equals Bettina von Arnim's social compassion and her powerful eloquence. She does not measure up to famous women novelists of world literature, like George Sand and George Eliot, with respect to powerful rhetoric, ease and nobility of imagination, also amount of literary output. But these women used their talents up more rapidly. More of the smaller number of her works might perhaps survive the test of time than might be the case with the works of these women.[1]

Many critics, however, put Ebner above Droste-Hülshoff,

whose work, it must be said objectively, she easily eclipsed both in terms of range of themes and literary output. From childhood on, Ebner was steeped in the German, French, and Russian classics. Her earliest and most influential literary and intellectual mentors were Friedrich Schiller and Ivan Turgenev. She succinctly reflects in her own writings and thoughts many of the themes and pronouncements of these literary models. In her earlier years as a writer she belonged in time and also in terms of style and ethos to Poetic Realism. Later in life, however, she became an eclectic, absorbing and reflecting also currents of the Naturalistic and Impressionistic schools of writing. She was well into her fifties when she achieved her first literary success. Until then she was known in only small literary circles. But success, as her first major biographer Anton Bettelheim informs us, did not spoil her. On the contrary, she became ever more productive and never lost her earlier sense of humility. Like no other contemporary writer, she was capable of uniting the ideals of her age: "kindness and strength."[2]

The year 1900, when Bettelheim's book on Ebner appeared—soon accompanied by another monograph, *Marie von Ebner-Eschenbach: Nach ihren Werken geschildert* (Marie von Ebner-Eschenbach: As Seen through Her Works), by Moritz Necker—was easily the year in which her popularity and esteem as a writer attained their highest peak. She had reached her seventieth year of life and received the greatest honors even from such a bastion of male chauvinism as the University of Vienna, which bestowed an honorary doctorate on her. She was the first woman so honored by this venerable and famous institution, the second-oldest, at the time, of German universities. In 1901, an Ebner-Eschenbach Prize for women writers was established, which was followed in 1910 by the founding of a Marie-von-Ebner-Eschenbach Fonds (Marie von Ebner-Eschenbach Foundation). From 1917 to 1920—the years in which the reputation of the authoress was still very high—three dissertations were written about her. These were followed by a great many others, reaching a statistical peak in 1930-1931, her anniversary years, and shortly thereafter. Although the interest of academicians in her declined substantially in subsequent years—reaching a low point from the mid-thirties to the end of the Second World War and a second nadir from 1950 to 1965—all in all as many as twenty-eight dissertations had been written on her by 1975.[3] Helga H. Harriman speaks of four additional dissertations dealing with Ebner-Eschenbach that appeared in the United States between 1977 and 1984.[4]

Yet beginning in the late 1920s and accelerating in the 1930s, a precipitous decline in her reputation set in. Aside from a trickle of dissertations in the following decades and the reprinting of some of her most successful stories for public school consumption relatively little interest was displayed in her oeuvre and literary achievements even in her native Austria. Only in the past decade and a half has there been a reemergence of interest in her life and works, leading to a number of studies and to the reissuance of some of her most popular works with updated commentaries, principally in Germany, East and West. There are at least two main reasons aside from the perennial bane of sexism that can be given to explain the downward course of her literary fame and her diminished reception. The first has to do with the scope of her work and its content, which were considered to be passé, dealing after all with conditions and situations in an Austrian empire that no longer existed. Thus literary historians would typically mention her as a woman writer of Moravian origin who, while representing and portraying primarily the Czech components of the Austro-Hungarian monarchy, was nonetheless loyal to the House of Habsburg.[5] Illustrative of this point is a summary of her work by the—in past decades—highly respected Germanist Josef Nadler, who speaks not only of the "limited" scope of her narratives, but also makes no mention of her literary endeavors in other genres:

> Her stories describe the entire monarchy and the entire age of Franz Joseph around the central focal point of Vienna, via Galicia, Transylvania, the Banat, back to Moravia. And they describe this domain and this era alternately from two perspectives, that of the castle and that of the village. The preferred world is the upper stratum of Austrian nobility: the preferred landscape [is] Moravia.[6]

The principal implication of this summary and other accounts of her literary achievements is that, since her stories focus primarily on the life of the old Austro-Hungarian aristocracy, any conflict portrayed in them brought about by social class and background must be dated. To be sure, World War One and the dissolution of both empires, the Austrian and the German, made her plots less interesting and relevant to the general reading public, who, as far as its educated elite was concerned, was not only preoccupied with concerns about national survival, but, in a purely literary sense, also partial to the new styles of post-Naturalism and—at least in the 1920s—literary Expressionism. By the same token, the readers and critics between the two world wars and in the period of the so-called cold war thereafter were also pressed by what they perceived to be more crucial matters than Marie Ebner's oeuvre presented to them. The ideals of humanism and loving kindness were in those epochs not a foremost concern. It must be added that, again from the purely stylistic point of view, Ebner contributed little that was strikingly new in the evolution of German letters. Her style—beholden as it is to literary Classicism, Romanticism, and to a great extent in later years also to Realism, Naturalism and Impressionism—is still pleasing to read today but hardly innovative, a fact that was and still is not lost on the literary and academic opinion makers, who, after all, exert a great amount of influence on the rating and standing, if not on the canonization, of past and present authors.

Other reasons for her declining reception are purely personal and political. They have to do with the Austrian aristocracy into which she was born and her upbringing. But this is not all. The rise of National Socialism to prominence and power in the German heartland did the most damage to her standing and reception prior to and during the era of the Third Reich. Ebner's liberal leanings, her political and personal embracing of a moderate and humane socialism devoid of all nationalistic fervor, and, above all her publicly expressed loathing of anti-Semitism, resulting in protracted and deep friendships with prominent Austrian and German Jews, were anathema to the National Socialists, who turned against her and her literary output. The above cited, rather mild critique of her works by Joseph Nadler is but a gentle reminder of the political pressures that the Nazi regime applied behind the scenes to change the public perception and to control the public mind in this and other instances.

Regrettably, some repercussions of this negative appraisal of her oeuvre are still with us today. They are, of course, no longer political in nature but much more subtle, giving Marie Ebner in effect the reputation of a sentimental, overly sensitive writer of limited background and purview. This criticism fails to understand that hers was the voice of one of the most significant and critical observers and commentators of her age. One can call her works as a whole strongly didactic. She meant them to convey and to instill in her readers, broadly speaking, positive modes of living. This, in turn, implied principally tolerance toward minorities such as Jews and other disadvantaged and abused people. Thus she wrote in her novella *Der Nebenbuhler* (The Rival) at a time when racial hatred and animosity toward Jews began to intensify in Austria: ". . . Racial hatred! . . . That is truly something awful and dumb in addition, as is any hatred which is focused on individuals instead of on the wrong they do. . . . Only love is wise . . ." (Hafis, 10:180).

Her reference to love as a higher, if not the highest, social goal as well as the compassionate and favorable depiction of Jews in her fiction confirm the deep rooting of her ethos in Judeo-Christian morality. This fact was not lost on the contemporary Jewish community. Hence the Jewish literary critic Klemperer noted in the *Allgemeine Zeitung des Judentums* (General Newspaper for Jews): "The fact that Marie Ebner chose Jews alongside Christians as representatives of her highest ideals of moral action is the strongest indicator of the fact that her religious sensibilities are not ensnared by religious prejudices."[7] Klemperer's point of view is expanded by Georg J. Plotke in a commemorative essay written early in 1917 in which he speaks ". . . of the fact that the internal feuds among races, classes, and ethnicities in the combined monarchy did attain a status of 'eternal peace' in her Slavo-Germanic dual nature:" (74). He extends his expansive analysis of her cosmopolitan worldview into an additional dimension:

> The redemption from opposites, from the forces opposed to progress, and the happy message of all-pervasive human love extend for this aristocratic woman also to the Jews. She had many Jewish friends not only in her personal life, but also tried in her writings to capture the Jews in a poetic fashion, [a people] who were especially unknown in her aristocratic circles on account of their social status and origin, and to have

them partake of the gospels of her grand worldview.
(75)

As an aristocrat Ebner was surely one of the most praisewor-
thy examples of a writer of the nobility practicing the age-old
adage of *noblesse oblige*. She was, of course, not alone in
this arena. It is no coincidence that the most outstanding
women writers of the nineteenth century preceding Marie von
Ebner-Eschenbach chronologically—Bettina von Arnim,
Annette von Droste-Hülshoff, and Louise von François—
were also members of the aristocracy following similar moral
guidelines. Their belonging to this still most privileged social
class ensured them intellectual liberties and freedoms of
action largely unattainable to lower-class women. It also
demonstrates that nobility of thought and action are no social
or ethical coincidence. Seen from this point of view, Ebner's
much praised "morality of love and compassion"[8] are the
result of both social rearing and personal convictions of the
highest order. Her ethos is reflected in all of her writings.
Thus her stories and dramatic fables are not just about
Moravia, imperial Vienna, Galicia, Transylvania, life in the
village and the castles of the privileged classes, as some of
her critics have previously held, but they also deal with the
plight of the Slavic minorities, the Jews, and the gypsies.
They decry the lower status of women and the agony of the
poverty-stricken masses. They condemn the abuse of old
people and of the young and—much ahead of her time—even
that of animals. It was not Marie Ebner's habit, however, to
preach social gospels in her creative writings. She merely
described. She showed. Although these matters were very
important to her, she put them on display in such a way that
her thoughtful readers would draw the—to her—correct con-
clusions and share her humanistic concerns. In so doing, she
also strikingly reflects and exposes the fraying social and

political compact that endangered the continuing existence of the Habsburg monarchy. This is perhaps one of the main reasons why many of her thoughtful contemporaries considered her to be the greatest living narrator in German literature of either sex. In Heyse's words, she used the privileges of her estate only "in order to rise above all traditional prejudices, to return an open mind vis-à-vis [all developments] above and below [her own social status], and to nurture and strengthen feelings of empathy for all that is filled with pain and loneliness in the world."[9]

Evidently, Marie Ebner is a woman writer whose agenda was set much higher than that of merely treading on male turf. Surely it was also not her intent to compete with E. Marlitt's and Nataly von Eschstruth's writings for popularity, whose best-selling novels *Goldelse* (Golden Elsa) and *Hofluft* (Court Air) border on *Trivialliteratur* (lowbrow literature). If general humanist concerns and reason are one approach to the potential problem areas weighing on her conscience and also bedeviling the society in which she lived, then the other avenue that her writings pursue is that of love. As much as her works reflect the all-pervasive power of thought and the word expressing it, they also exude the message of universal love. This powerful emotion, in effect, in its manifold manifestations extending even into the animal kingdom, is a recurring theme in all of her writings. Basically she aims at providing a balance in a nearly orthodox, classical sense. To this end she writes in a parable celebrating the desirable union of Wisdom and Kindness:

> Wisdom had to go on a cross-country trip and leave her favorite child, Kindness, for a while. When she returned home, she found her beautiful, quiet residence destroyed. . . . Her favorite, however, was gravely wounded and wandered in a shy and fright-

ened manner through the place, which had turned into a wilderness. . . .

"Oh, child," Wisdom said, filled with pain, "what becomes of our works, if I have to leave you to your own devices!"[10]

The oneness of reason and love is made even clearer in one of her aphorisms: "Reason and the heart have an excellent relationship with one another. The one often takes the place of the other in such a perfect way that it is difficult to decide which one of the two was acting" (Hafis, 11:104). This fusion of reason and love can also be extended into the social sphere where in Marie Ebner's view the absence of love on the part of the wealthy causes the social problems: "There would not be any social problems if the rich had been philanthropists in the first place" (Hafis, 11:129).

These aphoristic reflections of her innermost beliefs provide vivid examples of what sets Marie Ebner's work apart from that of most of her contemporaries. It is not only provocatively eclectic in method, but also graceful and aphoristic in style. Her mode of writing, in effect, can be said to be the opposite of oracular. Rather than adding or piling on one declarative statement after another beginning with the self, the I, as, for example, a Karl Emil Franzos would do in his writings, she withdraws, similar to Conrad Ferdinand Meyher, behind other personalities, a technique which betrays her dramatic origins without, however, diminishing the attractiveness of her narratives. In a letter to Paul Heyse she unveiled her concept of style: "I believe that all of us are consciously or subconsciously busy to gather the alphabet of a new language which, in time to come, will be spoken by morality. . . ."[11]

She practiced and perfected this "new style" principally in her aphorisms and parables. In writing them, she gave much thought to the essence of the former and ultimately defined this art form as the "last link of a long chain of thoughts" (20). She was also of the opinion that an aphorism had to provide the inner core of each and every one of her parables. Thus in her parable *Geschieden* (Divorced), she relates how Faith and Love were once happily married to each other. But after Faith ventures into the world on his own, he returns as an entirely different marriage partner. The author comments aphoristically: "Their union was a blessing; their disunity is a curse, and all of mankind feels its impact" (Hafis, 11:40). In a related parable, which Marie Ebner titled *Das Beste* (The Best) Love seems to turn the world. It may be the best that earth has to offer. But it can also be the worst, as the shocked creature Elanuh discovers, who visits the earth spirit Gaeus. The parable concludes with the words: "And before Gaeus could hold him back, Elanuh had escaped to his cool homeland" (Hafis, 11:50).

Marie Ebner knew about the dark side of love and its demons, as beholden as she was to this powerful human and universal emotion. In her parable *Besessen* (Possessed) she relates how a young man wastes his entire life because of a passionate and obsessive love for a goddess who continuously spurns him. In the end she admonishes him in a vein that brings Kafka's later parables to mind: "If lost, is it my fault? . . . Why are you pursuing me?—When did I call you?—Stop being of service to me, unwanted servant" (41). But essentially Marie Ebner wanted to believe in the basic good in man despite occasional doubts about his demeanor, as the following aphorism confirms: "All knowledge emanates from doubt and develops into belief."[12]

Had she lived longer, she would have doubtless also seen the very dark and destructive side of reason, which prior to World War I was well hidden from the people of her generation and had to await the coming of World War II to fully reveal itself, as her younger contemporary Stefan Zweig confirms in his autobiography *Die Welt von gestern* (The World of Yesterday):

> If I try to find an appropriate formula for the era prior to World War I, in which I grew up, I hope to be most precise when I say: It was the golden age of security. . . . In its liberal idealism, the nineteenth century was genuinely convinced that it was on a straight and direct path to the "best of all worlds." People looked down with contempt at earlier epochs with their wars, famines, and revolutions as times in which mankind was simply immature and not fully enlightened. . . . For a long time now we have repudiated for the sake of our own existence the religion of our fathers, their faith in a rapid and continuing ascending of humanity. That premature optimism seems banal to us, who have been taught so cruelly, in view of a catastrophe, which with a single blow threw us back by a thousand years of human efforts.[13]

Yet even decades before the atrocities of the two world wars and Hitler's genocidal policies, Marie Ebner was not naive enough to be so smitten with human rationality as not to have had some serious reservations about its alleged infinite potential for human progress. Her parable *Die Mussmenschen* (The Must People) not only makes this point clear, but it also projects an uncanny vision of potential social and political disasters ahead. It offers a view of a utopian society gone astray. A common criminal flees from jail and comes upon a people believing "in the repression of the human will" (Hafis, 11:9). They do not have laws and therefore need no judges to enforce them. Their society functions nonetheless, because everybody believes in the necessity of labor and in the supremacy of the social compact. Anyone transgressing these beliefs or not acting in accordance with them is considered to be mentally ill and has to present himself for medication and treatment in a public clinic:

> We humans, to be sure, are forced to live in a society, and since this is so, we have to try to make this socializing experience as beneficial as possible. Now experience has taught us that this can be done best, if peace, mutual respect, and goodwill prevail among us. Hence we based the total strength of our coerciveness on the realization of the stipulations of the general welfare. If in certain individuals an opposing coerciveness is observed, we can only look at it as being abnormal and must attempt to cure it. (14)

When the escaped criminal, who calls himself "a free man" (15), kills a warden practitioner in the clinic to which he is sent because of his refusal to work, he is condemned to death for being incurable. His final words before his execution are both accusatory and insightful: "You arrogant culture-apes, you are just as stupid as our people. Your coerciveness is our volition; your writers of prescriptions and our judges amount to the same" (16). The parable *Die Mussmenschen* is both a rejection of the potentially disastrous consequences of applying in a social setting Schopenhauer's powerful dictum on the denial of the will and an unbelievably early prognostication of the equally devastating potential of Marxist political philosophy of coercion being unleashed in human society. As Ebner sees it, the present social compact is far from being perfect but looming future developments have the potential of turning out much worse.

In the parable *Prometheus*, Marie Ebner expresses her

deepest doubts about the possibility of more benign conditions of existence for man and beast. In a distinct variation of the ancient myth, she shows a Prometheus who has been freed by the grace of the gods. There is but one condition. To uphold Zeus's previous oath to have him chained to a rock forever, he is obliged to wear a ring on which a chip of the rock of his martyrdom is fastened. He joins the gods in council, and they, in turn, listen to his words of wisdom. But the high promise of eternal bliss among immortals is rudely shattered when he feels compelled to look at the ring, which has become a gradually heavier and heavier burden:

> . . . again he lay shackled to the rock, and a dreadful beat of wings swished above his head. He felt the grip of claws of the vulture and the cruel pecking of the vulture's beak in his flesh.
>
> And the titan cried out in agony to the ruler of the world: "Powerless god, who can only pardon and not truly forgive one's sins! The recollection of my shame and expiation mocks your graciousness!"(18)

The author implies here in unmistakable terms that the universal ruler is as imperfect as his design. No matter how much one sacrifices or how hard one tries to make this a more humane world, the forces of inertia and restraint, once released, cannot be neutralized. Still, try one must.

These and other gems of insight provide ample testimony to the full scope of Marie Ebner's depth of intellectual perception and to her propensity for philosophical thought. Although her ethos has been called "typically female" by some analysts of her works, this sexist view did not withstand scholarly scrutiny and had to be amended. Thus Rudolf Latzke, a leading Austrian cultural and literary critic of previous decades, wrote about her ethos: "It is a genuine woman's ethos. It is uncomfortable for heroes and geniuses and in this sense similar to Grillparzer's. Only that Frau von Ebner-Eschenbach does not stop at Grillparzer's individualism, who sought inner peace only for himself, but she addresses social concerns."[14] To be sure, in her ethical views, Marie Ebner had also other teachers alongside Schiller and Grillparzer. First among them was doubtless the Russian writer Ivan Turgenev. He was, according to her own statement, her principal narrative model. Following Turgenev's lead, the authoress supported the downtrodden and ill-treated. Accordingly, both writers portray and describe the lives and fates of common people and expose the chasm between the haves and the have-nots in society.[15]

Marie von Ebner-Eschenbach, in fact, was in the forefront of those progressive and socially aware and active writers of the late nineteenth century who "propagate in their writings undogmatic private initiatives to alleviate human suffering and human want."[16] A contemporary observer of social affairs, Felice Ewart, wrote in a commemorative publication about Ebner's summer activities in St. Gilgen:

> The poorhouse is separated only by a narrow garden strip from Baroness Ebner's place. Three nuns look after the "needy." They take care of the small hospital and a kindergarten. When several times during the day Baroness Ebner happened to come by, the lives of the old and the young took a turn toward the better. I believe, they must have thought of her as a female Santa Claus in persona. She always had something she would give away, may it have been a little pack of tobacco, a piece of cake, a silver or copper coin—at rare occasions—just a kind word, a friendly smile.[17]

But it is important to remember in the overall context that

Marie Ebner's social behavior and her intellectuality did not result from structured early training. She was basically self-taught. Her autodidacticism became in the course of time second nature to her. She struggled practically all of her life to prove to herself and to the world that she, as a woman, had more than the proverbial and practical common sense condescendingly ascribed to her sex. Over the many years of her life, she had indeed developed a keen insight into the structure of the world within and without. She had accumulated wisdom about herself and the world around her. Hence she did not neglect to unveil the inner life of individuals and institutions. Her aphorisms and parables are ample proof of that.

It would also be a mistake to assume that the serious agenda of her beliefs and struggles barred her from developing a sense of humor and detachment, which is also usually not ascribed to writers of her sex. I have made reference to some of her hilarious narratives in preceding chapters. Yet her gentle humor and its tongue-in-cheek variety came to the fore in some of her aphorisms and parables as well. Thus she wrote: "A smart woman has millions of natural enemies:—all stupid men."[18] In a slightly more ironic manner which might not necessarily be appreciated by today's women's liberation movement, she chuckled: "When a woman learned how to read, the women's liberation movement was born" (36).

A good example of a combination of tongue-in-cheek humor and social criticism is her parabolic fairy tale, *Eine dumme Geschichte* (A Stupid Tale). It deals with the position of the woman in the home and in society. Formerly a virtuous wife was to serve her husband dutifully as does the wife of a knight, who considers removing her husband's boots to be one of her primary tasks in life:

Quietly and diligently she presided during the day

over the stove and the loom, and when the evening
descended, she climbed up to the loft and looked for
her itinerant master.

As soon as she beheld him, she waved her gold-
embroidered handkerchief and rushed down to the
courtyard of the castle to meet him. Then she and her
page accompanied the knight to his chambers, where
he threw himself onto his bear-pelt-covered bedstead,
thrust his legs at his gracious wife and exclaimed:
"Boots!"

And she approached him in loving servility and
removed her spouse's boots, which, depending on the
season, were covered with dust, mud, or snow. (Hafis,
11:23-24)

When the page, out of compassion for her, invents a ma-
chine—a "Stiefelknecht" (boot remover)—to do the chore for
her, she dismisses the idea and gets rid of both, the gadget
and him. Many centuries later this discarded device is by
chance discovered by the new owner of the castle. He rejects
it at first, his wife mocks it, and their children fight over it.
In the end, the perplexed, but condescending husband reflects
on the approaching liberation of women: "'Oh, dear wife, the
consequences are incalculable,' [he] sighed and—employed
the service of the boot remover" (28).

Marie von Ebner-Eschenbach's works are beholden to
outer reality, but they are also anchored in her own autobiography. Her writings—whether aphorisms, poems, parables,
dramas or narratives—are therefore not tethered by the rules
and precepts of fiction alone. These features, however, do not
diminish their attractiveness and their readability today.
Rather, the very opposite is the case. Guided as her fiction is
by the two principal forces of her inner makeup, reason and
love, many of her plots and fables have weathered the test of

time, style and public taste. Her works and their humanist message merit reading and discussion by an ever growing international public. There has, in effect been a remarkable reawakening of interest in her writings in the past decade and a half, witnessed not only by major investigations of her novelistic works, but also by new and expanded publications of many of her most popular narratives, her diaries, and her aphorisms. All of these activities confirm both a reaffirmation of her status as Austria's premier woman writer and—beyond that—as a major figure in Austrian and German literature irrespective of gender. All her life she fought gently and earnestly as well as with irony and humor not only against the moral obtuseness of her time and against the equivocating voices of public and private opinion makers, but also for a more just society and for more wholesome interpersonal relations. Having no children of her own, she thought of her readers as her children and her books as a garden of their delight and their edification. She spells out her innermost drive and goal in this endeavor in the motto to her volume of tales, *Miterlebtes* (Tales of Experience):

To move you, not to shock you, that is my desire.
To amuse some as well—if I can. (Hafis, 1:231)

NOTES AND REFERENCES

Chapter I: A Woman's Voice

1. Compare in this connection the long reign of Emperor Hirohito of Japan in most recent history. It extended over sixty-two years from 1926 to 1989, bridging the years leading up to the Second World War, those of the war itself as well as the post-wear period commonly called the Cold War. He was equally revered by his people even after Japan's devastating defeat and humiliation in 1944-1945, which forced him to give up his godlike stature but not his crown.

2. For further information read the introduction to Karl Emil Franzos's *Aus Halb-Asien,* a collection of vignettes and sociocritical essays dealing with the eastern parts of Europe in this period. Also see my book *Karl Emil Franzos, 1848-1904: Emancipator and Assimilationist* (New York, Bern, Frankfurt/Main, Paris: Peter Lang, 1990).

3. Johann Wolfgang Goethe, *Faust: Der Tragödie zweiter Teil, Goethes Sämtliche Werke: Jubiläume-Ausgabe,* ed. Erich Schmidt, 14 (Stuttgart and Berlin: Cotta, n.d.).

4. For a comprehensive discussion about the status and intellectual development of German-speaking women writers of that period see Susan Cocalis and Kay Goodman, editors, *Beyond the Eternal Feminine: Critical Essays on Women and German Literature,*

Stuttgarter Arbeiten zur Germanistik, 98 (Stuttgart: H.D. Heinz, 1982) and Ruth-Ellen B. Joeres and Mary Jo Maynes, editors, *German Women in the Eighteenth and Nineteenth Centuries: A Social and Literary History* (Bloomington: Indiana University Press, 1986).

5.   For an early but detailed discussion of this development see Helene Lange and Gertrud Bäumer, *Handbuch der Frauenbewegung,* 5 volumes (1901-1906).

6.   More comprehensive reading on this topic is provided by Edith Rigler, *Frauenliteratur und Frauenarbeit in Österreich vom ausgehenden 19. Jahrhundert bis zum Zweiten Weltkrieg* (Munich: E. Oldenbourg, 1976), pp. 37-53, and A. Harriet Anderson, "Feminism as a Vocation: Motives for Joining the Austrian Women's Movement," *Austrian Studies,* 1 (1990): 73-86.

7.   Compare "Preface," Marie von Ebner-Eschenbach, *Ausgewählte Werke,* ed. Josef Lackner (Linz: Österreichischer Verlag für Belletristik und Wissenschaft, 1947), p. 16.

8.   This essay was first published together with a number of other essays by contemporary writers about their first piece of creative writing by Karl Emil Franzos in a special edition of his literary magazine *Deutsche Dichtung.* The collection appeared later in book form entitled *Die Geschichte des Erstlingswerks.* Subsequent citations from this essay will be incorporated into the text.

9.   Marie von Ebner-Eschenbach, *Sämtliche Werke,* Hafis Edition, 12 (Leipzig: H. Fikentscher Verlag, 1928), p. 190. The translation from the original German text is the author's, as are all subsequent translations of future citations from this volume and all other volumes or texts of original source materials employed in

this study. All further quotations from the Hafis edition will be documented in the text. It may be of interest to note that *Meine Kinderjahre* is one of the first autobiographies in the German cultural sphere by a woman. The results of recent research into this area suggest that it is preceded by only two other similar works, the first of which was written by Fanny Lewald (born in 1811) and the other by Malwida von Meysenburg, (born 1816). For further details see Marie von Ebner-Eschenbach's *Autobiographische Schriften 1: Meine Kinderjahre. Aus meinen Kinder- und Lehrjahren,* ed. Christa-Maria Schmidt (Tübingen: Max Niemeyer, 1989), p. 229. Marie Ebner completed the text of her childhood recollections on March 12, 1905. It was first published in J. Rodenberg's *Deutsche Rundschau.* During her lifetime, three editions of *Kinderjahre* were printed. Her diaries of 1906 and 1907 are not extant.

10. Marie von Ebner-Eschenbach, *Ausgewählte Werke,* ed. Josef Lackner, p. 23.

11. This enlightened monarch, whose rule extended from 1765 to 1790, granted his subjects freedom of religion and also freed the peasants from serfdom.

12. This educational institution was named after the eighteenth-century Austrian empress Maria Theresa. It was an elite school for the sons of higher Austrian government officials and military officers. Its principal purpose was to train future civil servants for the empire.

13. See numbers 225, 226, 227, and 230. The well-known literary biographer Anton Bettelheim wrote a "Nachwort zu den 'Erinnerungen des Frhrn. Moriz v. Ebner-Eschenbach'" for the final installment.

14. He was one of the foremost Austrian physicists and

philosophers. Younger than Ebner-Eschenbach, he lived from 1838 to 1916. Mach strongly influenced philosophical positivism and the modern theory of logistics. Mach numbers as a measure of high speed, named after him, are universally employed.

15. *Beilagen zur Allgemeinen Zeitung,* Number 227:5 (Munich: October 5, 1899).

16. For a thorough account of the life and works of this important writer and publicist see Carl Steiner, *Karl Emil Franzos, 1848-1904: Emancipator and Assimilationist* (New York: Peter Lang, 1990).

17. This brilliant, but deeply troubled and unhappy son of Emperor Franz Joseph, who was to end his life by suicide, also entertained close intellectual relations with Franzos.

18. These writers were leading representatives of German Poetic Realism, a loosely knit literary movement in German letters of the second half of the nineteenth century owing its designation to Otto Ludwig, a dramatist, writer, and critic of the period.

19. This gifted member of a famous theater family wrote *Geschichte der deutschen Schauspielkunst.* It is still considered to be the most authoritative book on German actors and on the German stage prior to the twentieth century. See Simon Williams, *German Actors of the Eighteenth and Nineteenth Centuries* (Westport and London: Greenwood Press, 1985), pp. 177-178.

20. The free-lance writer Ferdinand von Saar—three years younger than Marie von Ebner-Eschenbach—was born in Vienna in 1833. Deeply troubled and depressed, the erstwhile officer committed suicide there in 1906. A realist writer and elegiac lyricist, he focuses on Viennese society and its psychological makeup in the sec-

ond half of the nineteenth century. In this sense, he has been called a precursor to Hugo von Hofmannsthal and Arthur Schnitzler. Saar's best lyrical output is contained in the volume *Wiener Elegien* (1893). Among his best-liked novellas is *Innocens* (1866), the author's first narrative, relating the story of abstinence and a friendship. *Schloss Kostenitz* (1893) tells a gripping tale of fleeting passion, redemption, and death.

21. This successful writer, dramatist, and journalist was born in Sprottau (Silesia) in 1806. His works were banished by edict of the Deutsche Bund in 1835 because of alleged immorality together with the writings of Heinrich Heine, Karl Gutzkow, Ludolf Wienbarg, and Theodor Mundt. All of their writings were grouped together under the heading of "Young Germany," an expression which had been used by Wienbarg in the first series of lectures published later under the title of *Ästhetische Feldzüge* (1834). Laube's most acclaimed work, the play *Die Karlsschüler* (1847), deals with Schiller's early experience in Stuttgart. From 1849 to 1867 Laube was the superintendent of the Burgtheater. He became the director of the Vienna Stadttheater in 1872 and continued in this function until 1880. Four years later he died in Vienna.

22. By way of an interesting parallel, it was also an ill-received comedy, his *Weh dem, der lügt* (1838), which caused Grillparzer in bitter resignation to discontinue his dramatic writings for publication and stage performance.

23. Of the same age as Marie von Ebner-Eschenbach—he was born in Berlin in 1830—he died in 1914 in Munich. He was one of the most prolific and versatile

authors of the period, writing narratives—principally
novellas, to the theoretical understanding of which he
also contributed with his much-discussed *Falkentheo-
rie*—dramas, verse epics, and poetry. In addition to
these, he had a number of translations to his credit
and worked as an editor for a while. His reputation
among his contemporaries was such that at the age of
eighty, in 1910, he received the Nobel Prize for
literature. After his death, however, interest in his
works, combining a romanticized thematic classicism
with realist descriptions and psychological insights,
rapidly declined.

24. Jews began to settle in Galicia in great numbers as
early as the twelfth century. In 1772, when it was incorporated into the Habsburg empire, the Jewish
inhabitants of the new province numbered 150,000
according to official statistics. By 1850, the number
had more than doubled, and in 1869 it rose to 575,000
or 10.6 percent of the total Galician population. For
additional details consult Arthur Eisenach, "Das
galizische Judentum während des Völkerfrühlings und
in der Zeit des Kampfes um seine Gleichberechtigung," *Zur Geschichte der Juden in den östliehen
Ländern der Habsburgmonarchie: Studia Judaica Austriaca*, 8 (Eisenstadt: Edition Roetzer, 1980).

25. The exact circumstances of this tragic event that
shook the Habsburg monarchy to its very foundations
and caused a permanent rift between the emperor and
his wife Elisabeth were so successfully hushed up at
the time and obfuscated that—in spite of many allegedly "sensational" disclosures over the past hundred
years—they will never be fully known. Yet the
damage that this tragedy at the highest level of state
inflicted upon the future political, social, ethnic, and

even psychological stability of Austria-Hungary is indisputable.

26. Compare in this connection Sigmund Freud's first psychoanalytical experiments and studies along these lines, which he conducted initially with Dr. Josef Breuer. See also *Marie von Ebner-Eschenbach und Dr. Josef Breuer: 1889-1916,* ed. Robert A. Kann (Vienna: Bergland, 1969).

27. August Sauer, *Gesammelte Reden und Aufsätze zur Geschichte der Literatur in Österreich und Deutschland* (Vienna: C. Fromme, 1903), p. 386.

28. *Heimatliteratur* reached its peak of popularity toward the end of the nineteenth century, when its folksy homespun stories of life in the country became part of a movement directed against the stark and grim depiction of decadent life spun out by the writers of Naturalism. It was resurrected in the Nazi era under the aegis of *Blut-und-Boden-Literatur.*

29. Ludwig Anzengruber, a dramatist and narrator who lived in Vienna all his life from 1839 to 1889, occupied a middle ground in his oeuvre between *Heimatliteratur* and representation of city life in the vein of literary naturalism. In most of his writings he expressed politically, socially, and culturally liberal and anticlerical views.

30. Marie von Ebner-Eschenbach, *Wer den Augenblick beherrscht, beherrscht das Leben: Aphorismen,* 3rd ed. (Steyr: Wilhelm Ennsthaler, 1985), p. 32. Future references to this volume will be given in the text under *Aphorismen.*

31. The oldest German university is that of Prague. It was founded in 1348 by Emperor Karl IV. The University of Vienna traces its founding back to the year 1365. Heidelberg is the oldest German university on German

soil today. Its founding year is 1385.

32. Viktor Adler founded the Austrian Social Democratic
     Party in 1888-89. He also became its leader. Of
     Jewish origin, he was born in Prague in 1852 and died
     in Vienna in 1918. Shortly before his death of natural
     causes, he was appointed to assume the post of the
     Austrian secretary of state.

33. See Helga H. Harriman, ed., *Seven Stories by Marie
     von Ebner-Eschenbach* (Columbia, South Carolina:
     Camden House, 1986), pp. xvi and xviii.

34. Reprinted in Adalbert Schmidt, *Dichtung und Dichter
     Österreichs im 19. und 20. Jahrhundert,* 1 (Salzburg
     and Stuttgart: Bergland-Buch, 1964), p. 173.

Chapter II: Dramatic Beginnings

1. The practice of showing operas on the stage of this
    theater stopped in the course of the nineteenth century,
    when the impressive building of the Wiener Hof- und
    Staatsoper at the Kärntner Ring on the one hand and
    the Volksoper near the Währinger Gürtel on the other
    provided permanent homes for Vienna's opera lovers.
    After the partial destruction of the Staatsoper toward
    the end of World War II, however, the Theater an der
    Wien became a temporary home for opera perform-
    ances again until the Staatsoper was restored.

2. It is noteworthy that some of Christoph Willibald
    Gluck's and also Mozart's most popular operas—
    Orfeo und Euridice, Alceste, Paride ed Elena of the
    former and *Die Hochzeit des Figaro, Don Giovanni,
    Die Zauberflöte* by the latter—were first performed
    here. See Hilde Haider-Pregler, *Theater und Schau-
    spielkunst in Österreich* (Vienna: Bundespressedienst,

n.d.), p. 64f.

3. Josef Schreyvogel (1768-1832), one of the most admired impresarios of his generation in the German language area—he worked for a while prior to his two appointments in Vienna under Goethe at the Weimar Hoftheater——was never officially given the title of director of the Burgtheater, because of his officially not sanctioned liberal views, which had driven him into exile to Weimar and Jena in the first place. His ill-conceived dismissal in 1832—the result of a base intrigue against him—led to his death.

4. For a more thorough discussion on this topic see Giulio Alliney, "Maria Stuart," *Kindlers Literatur Lexikon* (Zurich: Kindler, 1972), 7:6014-6036, from whose comprehensive article some of the above information has been excerpted.

5. Marie von Ebner-Eschenbach, *Maria Stuart in Schottland: Schauspiel in fünf Aufzügen* (Vienna: Ludwig Mayer, 1860), p. 9. All other documentation on this play will be given in the text. Also note that this edition contains pp. 1-25 and 39-64 only. Pp. 27-38 were deleted and the third act was, according to Ebner's own reference, rewritten entirely.

6. It should be noted, though, that Ludwig's critical and largely unfavorable analysis of Marie Ebner's play was not published during his lifetime. Found in his literary remains, it saw the light of publication after his death in 1865.

7. For more detailed information see *La Correspondence de Madame Roland avec les Desmoiselles Cannet* (2 vols., Paris, 1841) and *Lettres Autographes de Madame Roland, adressées a Bàncal des Issarts* (Paris, 1835).

8. Along professional lines, he also wrote and published

a number of so-called disquisitions on branches of industry.

9. Büchner's four-act play was written in 1835 prior to his flight to Strassburg, where he was forced to seek refuge from persecution as a political exile. It was first performed at the Belle-Alliance-Theater in Berlin on January 5, 1902.

10. Marie von Ebner-Eschenbach, *Marie Roland: Trauerspiel in fünf Aufzügen* (Vienna: J.B.Wallishausser, 1867), p. 5. All other references to this play are provided in the text.

11. See "Preface," Marie von Ebner-Eschenbach, *Ausgewählte Werke,* ed. Josef Lackner, p. 28.

12. Originally conceived as a play describing the tensions between the crown prince of Spain and his father, King Philip II, Schiller's Classical version shifted the emphasis from the personal problems of Don Carlos to the inner theme of human dignity and freedom.

13. The leading literary movement in Germany in the 70s and early 80s of the eighteenth century. Principally unfolding in the drama, its main characteristics are rejection of literary rationalism and its poetic rules on the one hand and espousal of emotionality and worship of genius on the other. Its most influential authors were young Goethe and young Schiller.

14. Marie von Ebner-Eschenbach, *Doktor Ritter: Dramatisches Gedicht in einem Aufzuge* (Vienna: F. Reitmann, 1869), p. 18. Further page references to this play will appear in the text.

15. Compare the introduction to *Ebner-Eschenbach: Werke in einem Band,* ed. Alice Koch (Berlin and Weimar: Aufbau-Verlag, 1982), p. ix.

16. Marie von Ebner-Eschenbach, *Die Veilchen: Lustspiel in einem Aufzuge* (Vienna: Wallishausser, 1877), p.

12.

17. Marie von Ebner-Eschenbach, *Ohne Liebe: Lustspiel in einem Akt* (Berlin: Bloch, n.d.), p. 36.
18. See Marie von Ebner-Eschenbach, *Aphorismen, Erzählungen, Theater,* ed. Romana Roček (Graz and Vienna: Böhlau, 1988), p. 589.
19. A leading Austro-German poet and writer of the turn of the century and a younger contemporary of Marie von Ebner-Eschenbach. He is still known and appreciated internationally as the author of *Jedermann* (1911) and as the librettist of Richard Strauss's best known operas.
20. Marie von Ebner-Eschenbach, "Das Waldfräulein," *Aphorismen, Erzählungen, Theater,* p. 540.
21. See *Ausgewählte Werke,* ed. Josef Lackner, p. 31.
22. Ibid.
23. Helga H. Harriman, p. xv.

Chapter III: Stories to Tell

1. Marie von Ebner-Eschenbach, *Wer den Augenblick beherrscht, beherrscht das Leben: Aphorismen,* p. 11. Marie Ebner always practiced what she preached. The most famous instance is the loving care she extended to Franz Grillparzer in his final years of life. Previously she had seen a father figure in him.
2. *Ausgewählte Werke,* ed. Josef Lackner, p. 35.
3. See Moritz Necker, *Marie von Ebner-Eschenbach: Nach ihren Werken geschildert* (Munich: Georg Müller, 1916), p. xviii.
4. Anton Bettelheim, *Marie von Ebner-Eschenbach und Julius Rodenberg* (Berlin: Gebrüder Paetel, 1920), p. 22.

5. Ibid., p. 23.
6. See August Sauer, *Gesammelte Reden und Aufsätz zur Geschichte der Literatur in Österreich und Deutschland* (Vienna: C. Fromme, 1903), p. 378.
7. Anton Bettelheim, *Marie von Ebner-Eschenbach: Biographische Blätter* (Berlin: Gebrüder Paetel, 1900), p. 159.
8. See Hans Otto Horch, *Auf der Suche nach der jüdischen Erzählliteratur: Die Literaturkritik der "Allgemeinen Zeitung des Judentums" (1837-1920)* (New York and Frankfurt/Main: Peter Lang, 1985). pp. 72-73.
9. For a detailed discussion of this novel see Carl Steiner, *Karl Emil Franzos (1848-1904): Enlightener and Assimilationist* (New York: Peter Lang, 1990), pp. 126-131.
10. Cf. *Gesammelte Reden*, p. 382.
11. High, usually honorary title of imperial civil servant, which was also extended to his wife or widow.
12. Compare Franzos's at that time very popular novels: *Der Wahrheitssucher* 1893), *Der Präsident* (1884), *Die Reise nach dem Schicksal* (1885), *Ein Kampf ums Recht* (1882), and *Die Schatten* (1888). They reflect in themes and content Marie Ebner's sarcastic remarks.

Chapter IV: The Novelistic Works

1. See in this connection his *Die Theorie des Romans* (1916 and 1963) and his *Der historische Roman* (1955).
2. The three principal thirteenth-century German epic writers of what has frequently been called the first golden age of German literature. The two most

famous courtly epics of this period are Wolfram von Eschenbach's *Parzival* and Gottfried von Strassburg's *Tristan und Isolde*.

3. M. Rosa Doyle, *Catholic Atmosphere in Marie von Ebner-Eschenbach: Its Use as a Literary Device* (New York: AMS Press, n.d.), p. 295.

4. See Marie von Ebner-Eschenbach, *Kritische Texte und Deutungen*, 2, *Božena*, ed. Kurt Binneberg (Bonn: Bouvier, 1980) p. 295.

5. This citation is taken from Kurt Binneberg's *Božena* edition, p. 207. Subsequent references to this volume will be cited in the text.

6. Reprinted in Marie von Ebner-Eschenbach, *Kritische Texte und Deutungen*, 3, *Das Gemeindekind*, ed. Rainer Baasner (Bonn: Bouvier, 1983), p. 189. All other references to this book will be given in the text.

7. Compare Paul Wiegler, *Geschichte der deutschen Literatur* (Berlin, 1930), 2:653.

8. See Edgar Gross, "Nachwort," *Unsühnbar* (Munich: Nymphenburger Verlagsbuchhandlung, 1957), p. 266.

9. There is documentary evidence that a spiritualist craze engulfed the highest aristocratic circles in Austria in those days. Even the heir to the Austrian throne, Crown Prince Rudolf, who was highly frustrated by his inability to effect political change, was said to have attended spiritual séances.

10. See Marie von Ebner-Eschenbach, *Kritische Texte und Deutungen*, 1, *Unsühnbar*, ed. Burkhard Bittrich (Bonn: Bouvier, 1978), pp. 236-245. Further documentation about this edition will be cited in the text.

11. A pseudonym for Florentine Galliny (1845-1913), journalist essayist, and literary review critic.

12. Compare this author's developmental novel *Der Wahrheitssucher*. A detailed account of this novel is

given in *Karl Emil Franzos, 1848-1904*, pp. 146-154.
13. See *Ausgewählte Werke*, p. 63.

Chapter V: The Humanist Message

1. *Gesammelte Reden*, p. 393.
2. See Bettelheim, *Marie von Ebner-Eschenbach: Biographische Blätter*, p. 229.
3. For a detailed discussion on this matter see Alexandra Unterholzner's unpublished dissertation "Marie von Ebner-Eschenbach: Eine Analyse der Form der Rezeption ihres Werkes." (Innsbruck, 1978), p. 207ff.
4. Harriman, p. xxiii.
5. Compare Claudio Magris, *Der habsburgische Mythos in der österreichischen Literatur* (Salzburg: Otto Müller, 1966), p. 156.
6. Josef Nadler, *Literaturgeschichte des deutschen Volkes*, 4th ed. (Berlin: Propyläen Verlag, 1941), 4:164.
7. Horch, p. 74.
8. See Fritz Martini, *Deutsche Literatur im bürgerlichen Realismus* (Stuttgart: Metzler, 1962), p. 486.
9. Reprinted in Bettelheim, *Biographische Blätter*, p. 240
10. See Marie von Ebner-Eschenbach, *Letzte Worte: Aus dem Nachlass*, ed. Helene Bucher (Vienna: Rikola, 1923), p. 292.
11. Marie von Ebner-Eschenbach, *Weisheit des Herzens*, ed. Heinz Rieder (Graz and Vienna: Stiasny, 1958), p. 13.
12. *Aphorismen*, p. 63. This aphorism also provides irrefutable proof of her strong humanistic worldview.
13. Stefan Zweig, *Die Welt von gestern* (Frankfurt/Main: S. Fischer, 1955), pp. 13-16.

14. Rudolf Latzke, "Die Ethik der Marie von Ebner-Eschenbach," *Quelle* (1931), 3:6.

15. Compare Ingeborg Geserick, "Marie von Ebner-Eschenbach und Ivan Turgenev," *Zeitschrift für Slawistik*, 1 (1956), 1:43-64, and Anton Bettelheim, *Marie von Ebner-Eschenbach: Wirken und Vermächtnis* (Leipzig, 1920), p. 146.

16. Burkhard Bittrich, *Die Anfänge der sozialen Erzählung in Österreich* (Salzburg and Munich: Anton Pustet, 1979), p. 17.

17. Ibid., p. 15.

18. *Aphorismen*, p. 44. This funny remark with its play on words also provides a brilliant refutation of such highly biased and commonly used German adjectives as "herr·lich" (grand, magnificent) and "däm·lich" (stupid, silly).

A SELECT BIBLIOGRAPHPY

The works and publications listed below were used in this study.

A. Works by Marie von Ebner-Eschenbach

Aphorismen. Afterword by Karl Krolow. Frankfurt/Main: Insel, 1986.

Aphorismen, Erzählungen, Theater. Ed. Roman Roček. Graz and Vienna: Böhlau, 1988.

Aus Franzensbad: Sechs Episteln von keinem Propheten. Reprint of 1858 edition. Ed. and commentator Karlheinz Rossbacher. Vienna: Österreichischer Bundesverlag, 1985.

Ausgewählte Werke. Ed. Josef Lackner. Linz: Österreichischer Verlag für Belletristik und Wissenschaft, 1947.

"Aus meinen Kinder- und Lehrjahren." Ed. Karl Emil Franzos. *Die Geschichte des Erstlingswerks.* Leipzig: Adolf Titze, 1894.

Autobiographische Schriften. Vol. 1. *Meine Kinderjahre. Aus meinen Kinder- und Lehrjahren.* Ed. Christa-Maria Schmidt. Tübingen: Niemeyer, 1989.

Bertram Vogelweid. 2nd ed. Berlin: Gebrüder Paetel, 1901.

Doktor Ritter: Dramatisches Gedicht in einem Aufzuge. Vienna: F. Reitmann, 1869.

Erinnerungen: Meine Kinderjahre. Meine Erinnerungen an Grillparzer. Munich: Nymphenburger Verlagsbuchhandlung, 1959.

Erzählungen. Autobiographische Schriften. Ed. Johannes Klein. Vienna: Deutsche Buch-Gemeinschaft, no date.

Die Freiherren von Gemperlein. Afterword by Fritz Böttger. Berlin: Verlag der Nation, 1983.

Das Gemeindekind. Vienna: Buchgemeinschaft Donauland, no date.

Das Gemeindekind. Novellen. Aphorismen. Ed. Johannes Klein. Vienna: Deutsche Buch-Gemeinschaft, no date.

Kleine Romane. Ed. Johannes Klein. Vienna: Deutsche Buch-Gemeinschaft, no date.

Krambambuli und andere Novellen. Vienna: Buchgemeinschaft Donauland, 1957.

Kritische Texte und Deutungen. Vol. 1. *Unsühnbar.* Ed. Burkhard Bittrich. Bonn: Bouvier, 1978.

Kritische Texte und Deutungen. Vol. 2. *Božena.* Ed. Kurt Binneberg. Bonn: Bouvier, 1980.

Kritische Texte und Deutungen. Vol. 3. *Das Gemeindekind.* Ed. Rainer Baasner. Bonn: Bouvier, 1983.

Kritische Texte und Deutungen. Vol. 4. *Meine Kinderjahre.* Ed. Christa-Maria Schmidt. Tübingen: Niemeyer, 1989.

Kritische Texte und Deutungen. Vol. 5. Meine Erinnerungen an Grillparzer. Christa-Marie Schmidt. Tübingen: Niemeyer, 1989.

Letzte Worte: Aus dem Nachlass. Ed. Helene Bucher. Vienna: Rikola, 1923.

Margarete. 5th ed. Stuttgart and Berlin: Cotta, 1901.

Maria Stuart in Schottland: Schauspiel in fünf Aufzügen. Vienna: Ludwig Mayer, 1860.

Marie Roland Trauerspiel in fünf Aufzügen. Vienna: J.B. Wallishausser, 1867.

Der Nachlass der Marie von Ebner-Eschenbach in vier Bänden. Ed. Heinz Rieder. Vol. 1. *Bei meinen Landsleuten.* Vienna: Agathon, 1948.

Ohne Liebe: Lustspiel in einem Akt. Berlin: Bloch, no date.

Oversberg: Aus dem Tagebuch des Volontärs Ferdinand Binder. Vienna: C. Daberkow, no date.

Sämtliche Werke: Hafis-Ausgabe. 12 volumes. Leipzig: H. Fikentscher Verlag, H. Schmidt and C. Günther, 1928.

Tagebücher I: 1862–1869. Ed. Karl Konrad Polheim. Tübingen: Niemeyer, 1989.

The Two Countesses. Translated by Mrs. Waugh. London: T. Fisher Unwin, 1893.

Unsühnbar. Munich: Nymphenburger Verlagsbuchhandlung, 1957.

Die Veilchen: Lustspiel in einem Aufzuge. Vienna: J.B. Wallishausser, 1877.

Weisheit des Herzens. Ed. Heinz Rieder. Graz and Vienna: Stiasny, 1958.

Wer den Augenblick beherrscht, beherrscht das Leben: Aphorismen. 3rd ed. Steyr: Wilhelm Ennsthaler, 1985.

Werke in einem Band. Ed. Alice Koch. Berlin and Weimar: Aufbau-Verlag, 1982.

B. Letter Collections

Briefwechsel zwischen Ferdinand von Saar und Marie von Ebner-Eschenbach. Ed. Heinz Kindermann. Vienna: Wiener Bibliophilen Gesellschaft, 1957.

Marie von Ebner-Eschenbach und Dr. Josef Breuer: 1889–1916. Ed. Robert A. Kann. Vienna: Bergland, 1969.

Marie von Ebner-Eschenbach und Gustav Frenssen: Ein Briefwechsel. Vienna: Carl Fromme, 1917.

C. Published and Unpublished Studies about Marie von Ebner-Eschenbach

"Aus den Erinnerungen des k.k. Feldmarschalleutnants a. D. Moriz Frhrn. v. Ebner-Eschenbach." *Beilagen zur Allgemeinen Zeitung.* Munich: Nrs. 225, 226, 227 (Oct, 3, 4, 5).

Benesch, Kurt. *Die Frau mit den hundert Schicksalen: Das Leben der Marie von Ebner-Eschenbach.* Vienna and Munich: Österreichischer Bundesverlag, 1966.

Bettelheim, Anton. *Marie von Ebner-Eschenbach: Biographische Blätter.* Berlin: Gebrüder Paetel, 1900.

____. *Marie von Ebner-Eschenbach und Julius Rodenberg.* Special edition of *Deutsche Rundschau.* Berlin: Gebrüder Paetel, 1920.

____. "Nachwort zu den 'Erinnerungen des Frhrn. Moriz v. Ebner-Eschenbach.'" *Beilage zur Allgemeinen Zeitung.* Number 230. Munich; Oct. 9, 1899.

Consbruch, Helene. "Das Kind bei Marie Ebner-Eschenbach." *Die Lese.* 9, 1 (1917): 224–225.

Fischer, Erika. "Marie von Ebner-Eschenbach und ihr Verhältnis zur Frauenfrage." Reprint in possession of the Wiener Stadt- und Landesbibliothek. No publisher, No date.

____. *Soziologie Mährens in der zweiten Hälfte des 19. Jahrhunderts als Hintergrund der Werke Marie von Ebner-Eschenbachs.* Leipzig: Ernst Wunderlich, 1939.

Geserick, Ingeborg. "Marie von Ebner-Eschenbach und Ivan Turgenev." *Zeitschrift für Slawistik.* 1, 1 (1956): 43–64.

Gladt, Karl. "Ein Skizzenbuch der Marie von Ebner-Eschenbach." *Librarium: Zeitschrift der Schweizerischen*

Bibliophilen—Gesellschaft, 2 (1967):3–18.

Gögler, Maria. *Die pädagogischen Anschauungen der Marie von Ebner-Eschenbach.* Leipzig: Kurt Vieweg, no date.

Grengg, M. and Dora Siegl. *Österreichische Dichterfürstin: Marie von Ebner-Eschenbach.* Prague, Vienna, Leipzig: A. Haase, no date.

Harriman, Helga H. Ed. *Seven Stories by Marie von Ebner-Eschenbach.* Columbia (South Carolina): Camden House, 1986.

Koller, Albert. *Studien zu M. von Ebner-Eschenbach.* Inaugural-Dissertation. Hamburg: Lütcke and Wulff, 1920.

Kubelka, Margarete. *Marie von Ebner-Eschenbach: Porträt einer Dichterin.* Bonn: Bund der Vertriebenen, 1982.

Latzke, Rudolf. "Die Ethik der Marie von Ebner-Eschenbach." *Quelle* (1931), 3: 1–15.

___. "Marie von Ebner-Eschenbach und Iwan Turgenjew." *Pädagogischer Führer* (1935). 4: 402–412.

Muehlberger, Josef. *Marie von Ebner-Eschenbach: Eine Studie.* Leipzig: Frankenstein and Wagner, 1930.

Muerdel-Dormer, Lore. "Tribunal der Ironie: Marie von Ebner-Eschenbachs Erzählung 'Er lasst die Hand küssen.'" *Modern Austrian Literature.* 9, 2 (1976): 86–97.

Necker, Moritz. "Marie von Ebner-Eschenbach: Ein literarisches Charakterbild." *Deutsche Rundschau.* 12 (1890): 338–357.

___. *Marie von Ebner-Eschenbach: Nach ihren Werken geschildert.* Leipzig and Berlin: Georg Heinrich Mayer, 1900.

Offergeld, Kaethe. *Marie von Ebner-Eschenbach: Untersuchungen über ihre Erzähltechnik.* Dissertation. Munster: Westfälische Vereinsdruckerei, 1917.

Radke, M.F. "Das Tragische in den Erzählungen von Marie

von Ebner-Eschenbach." Unpublished Dissertation.
University of Marburg, 1918.

Riemann, Else. *Zur Psychologie und Ethik der Marie von Ebner-Eschenbach.* Hamburg: H.O. Persiehl, 1913.

Sahánek, Stanislaus. "Das tschechische Dorf bei Marie von Ebner-Eschenbach." *Xenia Pragensia* (1929): 114.

"Sammlung 'Dichter'": Konvolut von Broschüren und Zeitungsausschnitten von und über Marie von Ebner-Eschenbach. Wiener Stadt- und Landesbibliothek, Nr. 57–60.

Unterholzner, Alexandra. "Marie von Ebner-Eschenbach: Eine Analyse der Form der Rezeption ihres Werkes." Unpublished Dissertation. Innsbruck, 1978.

Vogelsang, Hans. "Marie von Ebner-Eschenbachs Weltbild und Menschenideal: Zum 50. Todestag der Dichterin am 12. März 1966." *Österreich in Geschichte und Literatur.* 10 (1966), 3: 122–132.

Was bedeutet Marie von Ebner-Eschenbach für uns Erzieherinnen der Jugend? Rede zur Gedenkfeier für Marie von Ebner-Eschenbach, gehalten am 31. März 1916, Vienna: Franz Deuticke, no date.

D. Works of General Reference

Anderson, Harriet. "Feminism as a Vocation: Motives for Joining the Austrian Women's Movement." *Austrian Studies.* 1 (1990): 73–86.

_____. Utopian Feminism: *Women's Movements in Fin-de-Siècle Vienna.* New Haven: Yale University Press, 1992.

Blackwell, Jeannine and Susanne Zantop. Ed. *Bitter Healing: German Women Writers from 1700 to 1830.* Lincoln and London: University of Nebraska Press, 1990.

Bittrich, Burkhard. Ed. *Anfänge der sozialen Erzählung in Österreich.* Salzburg and Munich: Pustet, 1979.

Böttcher, Kurt et al. *Geschichte der deutschen Literatur von 1830 bis zum Ausgang des 19. Jahrhunderts.* Berlin: Volk und Wissen volkseigener Verlag, 1975.

Bramkamp, Agathe C. *Marie von Ebner-Eschenbach: The Author, Her Time, and her Critics.* Bonn: Bouvier, 1990.

Cocalis, Susan and Kay Goodman. Ed. *Beyond the Eternal Feminine: Critical Essays on Women and German Literature.* Stuttgarter Arbeiten zur Germanistik. 98. Stuttgart: H.D. Heinz, 1982.

Devrient, Eduard. *Geschichte des deutschen Schauspiels.* Berlin: Elsner, 1905.

Eisenach, Arthur. "Das galizische Judentum während des Völkerfrühlings und in der Zeit des Kampfes um seine Gleichberechtigung." *Zur Geschichte der Juden in den östlichen Ländern der Habsburgmonarchie: Studia Judaica Austriaca.* Eisenstadt: Edition Roetzer, 1980.

Glaser, Hermann. Ed. *The German Mind of the 19th Century.* New York: Continuum, 1981.

Goethe, Johann Wolfgang. *Goethes sämtliche Werke: Jubiläums-Ausgabe.* Ed. Erich Schmidt. 14. Stuttgart and Berlin: Cotta, no date.

Janik, Allan and Stephen Toulmin. *Wittgenstein's Vienna.* New York: Simon and Schuster, 1973.

Joeres, Ruth–Ellen and Mary Jo Maynes. Ed. *German Women in the Eighteenth and Nineteenth Centuries: A Social and Literary History.* Bloomington: Indiana University Press, 1986.

Johann, Ernst and Jörg Junker. *German Cultural History of the Last Hundred Years.* Munich: Nymphenburger Verlagsbuchhandlung, 1970.

Kindlers Literatur Lexikon. Chief editors Gert Woerner, Rolf Geisler, and Rudolf Radler, 12 volumes. Zurich: Kindler, 1972.

Magris, Claudia. *Der habsburgische Mythos in der österreichischen Literatur.* Salzburg: Otto Müller, 1966.

Meyer, Richard Moritz. *Die deutsche Literatur des neunzehnten Jahrhunderts.* 3rd ed. Berlin: Georg Bondi, 1906.

Rigler, Edith. *Frauenleitbild und Frauenarbeit in Österreich vom ausgehenden 19. Jahrhundert bis zum Zweiten Weltkrieg.* Vienna: Verlag für Geschichte und Politik, 1976.

Sauer, August. *Gesammelte Reden und Aufsätze zur Geschichte der Literatur in Österreich und Deutschland.* Vienna: C. Fromme, 1903.

Schmidt, Adalbert. *Dichtung und Dichter Österreichs im 19. und 20. Jahrhundert.* 1. Salzburg and Stuttgart: Bergland-Buch, 1964.

Weiland, Daniela. *Geschichte der Frauenemanzipation in Deutschland und Österreich.* Dusseldorf: Econ, 1983.

Williams, Simon. *German Actors of the Eighteenth and Nineteenth Centuries: Idealism, Romanticism, and Realism.* Westport and London: Greenwood Press, 1985.

MARIE VON EBNER-ESCHENBACH'S MAJOR WORKS: A CHRONOLOGY

1858   *Aus Franzensbad:* Sechs Episteln von keinem Propheten

1860   *Maria Stuart in Schottland:* Schauspiel in fünf Aufzügen

1862   *Die Veilchen:* Lustspiel in einem Aufzuge

1867–68   *Das Waldfräulein:* Lustspiel

1868   *Marie Roland:* Trauerspiel in fünf Aufzügen

1869   *Doktor Ritter:* Dramatisches Gedicht in einem Aufzuge

1872   *Die Prinzessin von Banalien*

1875   *Erzählungen*
        Ein Spätgeborener
        Chlodwig
        Die erste Beichte
        Die Grossmutter
        Ein Edelmann

1876   *Božena*

1877   *Nach dem Tode*

1879   *Die Freiherren von Gemperlein*

1880   *Aphorismen*
        Lotti, die Uhrmacherin

1881   *Neue Erzählungen*
        (Die Freiherren von Gemperlein
        Lotti, die Uhrmacherin
        Nach dem Tode)

1883   *Dorf- und Schlossgeschichten*

WRITINGS BY
MARIE VON EBNER-ESCHENBACH
IN ENGLISH TRANSLATION

The Two Countesses. Trans. Ellen Waugh. New York: Cassel, 1893.

"Krambambuli." Trans. A. Coleman. *The German Classics: Masterpieces of German Literature.* Ed. Kuno Francke, 13 (1914), 417-428.

Selected Austrian Short Stories: "Jakob Szela," "The Finch." Trans. and ed. Marie Busch. Freeport (New York): Books for Libraries Press, 1971.

"Talent is Only Another Word for Power: A Letter from Marie von Ebner-Eschenbach (1830-1916)." Trans. Helga N. Harriman. *Women's Studies International: A Supplement of the Women's Studies Quarterly,* 3 (1984), 17-18.

Seven Stories by Marie von Ebner-Eschenbach: "Krambambuli," "Jakob Szela," "Countess Muschi," "Countess Paula," "The Wake," "The Finch," "The Travelling Companions." Trans. and ed. Helga H. Harriman. Columbia (South Carolina): Camden House, 1986.

NAME AND TITLE INDEX

Sand, George, 182
Scheherazade, 101-102
Schiller, Friedrich, 20, 21, 24, 33, 34, 36, 41, 61, 65, 68-69, 88, 89-90, 99, 149, 183
  Maria Stuart, 33, 65, 68-69
  Die Räuber, 89-90
Schopenhauer, Arthur, 193
Schwarzenberg, Felix von, 27
Shakespeare, William, 20, 33
Stifter, Adalbert, 123, 147
  Abdias, 123
  Nachsommer, 147
  Witiko, 147
Storm, Theodor, 40, 113

T
Tolstoy, Lev Nikolayevich, 122, 165-166
  Anna Karenina, 165, 166
Turgenev, Ivan Sergeyevich, 38, 41-42, 104, 141, 183, 195
  Fathers and Sons, 141
  First Love, 141
  Komets Chertapkhanova, 41-42
  Mumu, 41
  Smoke, 141
  Virgin Soil, 141

V
Vockel, Marie von, 14, 15, 17

W
Wellen, Joseph von, 32, 87-88, 113, 182
Wilhelm II, 46

Z
Zedlitz, Josef Christian von, 19, 96
  Loblied auf den Rhein, 19
  Das Waldfräulein, 96
Zweig, Stefan, 192
  Die Welt von gestern, 192

ARIADNE PRESS
Translation Series:

February Shadows
By Elisabeth Reichart
Translated by Donna L. Hoffmeister
Afterword by Christa Wolf

Night Over Vienna
By Lili Körber
Translation by Viktoria Hertling
& Kay M. Stone. Commentary by
Viktoria Hertling

The Cool Million
By Erich Wolfgang Skwara
Translated by Harvey I. Dunkle
Preface by Martin Walser
Afterword by Richard Exner

Buried in the Sands of Time
Poetry by Janko Ferk
English/German/Slovenian
English Translation by H. Kuhner

Puntigam or The Art of Forgetting
By Gerald Szyszkowitz
Translated by Adrian Del Caro
Preface by Simon Wiesenthal
Afterword by Jürgen Koppensteiner

Negatives of My Father
By Peter Henisch
Translation and Afterword
by Anne C. Ulmer

On the Other Side
By Gerald Szyszkowitz
Translated by Todd C. Hanlin
Afterword by Jürgen Koppensteiner

The Slackers and Other Plays
By Peter Turrini
Translation and Afterword
by Richard S. Dixon

The Baron and the Fish
By Peter Marginter
Translation and Afterword
by Lowell A. Bangerter

I Want to Speak
The Tragedy and Banality
of Survival in
Terezin and Auschwitz
By Margareta Glas-Larsson
Edited and with a Commentary
by Gerhard Botz
Translated by Lowell A. Bangerter

The Works of Solitude
By György Sebestyén
Translation and Afterword
by Michael Mitchell

Krystyna
By Simon Wiesenthal
Translated by Eva Dukes

Deserter
By Anton Fuchs
Translation and Afterword
by Todd C. Hanlin

From Here to There
By Peter Rosei
Translation and Afterword
by Kathleen Thorpe

The Angel of the West Window
By Gustav Meyrink
Translated by Michael Mitchell

Relationships
An Anthology of Contemporary
Austrian Literature
Selected and with an Introduction
by Adolf Opel

Three Late Plays
By Arthur Schnitzler
Translation and Afterword
G.J. Weinberger

Professor Bernhardi and Other Plays
By Arthur Schnitzler
Translation G.J. Weinberger
Afterword Jeffrey B. Berlin

Translations:

The Bengal Tiger
By Jeannie Ebner
Translation and Afterword
by Lowell A. Bangerter

Three Flute Notes
By Jeannie Ebner
Translation and Afterword
by Lowell A. Bangerter

Farewell to Love and Other
Misunderstandings
By Herbert Eisenreich
Translation and Afterword
by Renate Latimer

The Sphere of Glass
By Marianne Gruber
Translation and Afterword
by Alexandra Strelka
Preface by Joseph P. Strelka

A Man Too White
By György Sebestén
Translation and Afterword
by Michael Mitchell

The Green Face
By Gustav Meyrink
Translated by Michael Mitchell

The Ariadne Book of Austrian Fantasy
The Meyrink Years 1890-1930
Edited and translated
by Michael Mitchell

Walpurgisnacht
By Gustav Meyrink
Translated by Michael Mitchell

On the Wrong Track
By Milo Dor
Translated by Jerry Glenn
and Jennifer Kelley

Night Train
By Friederike Mayröcker
Translation and Afterword
by Beth Bjorklund

Memories With Trees
By Ilse Tielsch
Translation and Afterword
by David Scrase

Return to the Center
By Otto von Habsburg
Translated by Carvel de Bussy

View from a Distance
By Lore Lizbeth Waller

Five Plays
By Gerald Szyszkowitz
Translated by Todd Hanlin, Heidi
Hutchinson and Joseph McVeigh

Anthology of Contemporary Austrian
Folk Plays
By Veza Canetti, Peter Preses &
Ulrich Becher, Felix Mitterer, Gerald
Szyszkowitz, Peter Turrini
Translation and Afterword
by Richard Dixon

The Condemned Judge
By Janko Ferk
Translation and Afterword
by Lowell A. Bangerter

Thomas Bernhard and His
Grandfather: "Our Grandfathers
Are Our Teachers."
By Caroline Markolin
Translated by Petra Hartweg

The Convent School
By Barbara Frischmuth
Translated by
Gerald Chapple and James B. Lawson

The Calm Ocean
By Gerhard Roth
Translated by Helga Schreckenberger
and Jacqueline Vansant

Remembering Gardens
by Kurt Klinger
Translated by Harvey I. Dunkle

ARIADNE PRESS

Studies in Austrian Literature, Culture and Thought

Major Figures of
Modern Austrian Literature
Edited and Introduced
by Donald G. Daviau

Major Figures of Turn-of-the-Century
Austrian Literature
Edited and Introduced
by Donald G. Daviau

Austrian Writers and the
Anschluss: Understanding the
Past—Overcoming the Past
Edited and Introduced
by Donald G. Daviau

Introducing Austria
A Short History
By Lonnie Johnson

Coexistent Contradictions
Joseph Roth in Retrospect
Edited by
Helen Chambers

The Verbal and Visual Art of
Alfred Kubin
By Phillip H. Rhein

Kafka and Language
In the Stream of
Thoughts and Life
By G. von Natzmer Cooper

Robert Musil and the Tradition
of the German Novelle
By Kathleen O'Connor

Blind Reflections:
Gender in Elias Canetti's
Die Blendung
By Kristie A. Foell

Conversations with Peter Rosei
By Wilhelm Schwarz

Austria in the Thirties
Culture and Politics
Edited by Kenneth Segar
and John Warren

Stefan Zweig:
An International Bibliography
By Randolph J. Klawiter

Austrian Foreign Policy
Yearbook
Report of the Austrian Federal
Ministry for Foreign Affairs
for the Year 1990

Quietude and Quest
Protagonists and Antagonists in
the Theater, on and off Stage
As Seen Through the Eyes of
Leon Askin
Leon Askin and C. Melvin Davidson

"What People Call Pessimism":
Sigmund Freud, Arthur Schnitzler
and Nineteenth-Century
Controversy at the University
of Vienna Medical School
By Mark Luprecht

Arthur Schnitzler and Politics
By Adrian Clive Roberts

Structures of Disintegration
Narrative Strategies in
Elias Canetti's Die Blendung
By David Darby

Of Reason and Love
The Life and Work of Marie von
Ebner-Eschenbach
By Carl Steiner

Franz Kafka:
A Writers Life
By Joachim Unseld